Every Good
Thing

SATISFYING YOUR
HUNGER FOR GOD

MIKE TUCKER

Autumn
House® Publishing
www.autumnhousepublishing.com
A Division of REVIEW AND HERALD® PUBLISHING
Since 1861

Published by Autumn House® Publishing, a division of Review and Herald® Publishing, Hagerstown, MD 21741-1119

Autumn House® titles may be purchased in bulk for educational, business, fund-raising, or sales promotional use. For information, please e-mail SpecialMarkets@reviewandherald.com.

Autumn House® Publishing publishes biblically based materials for spiritual, physical, and mental growth and Christian discipleship.

The author assumes full responsibility for the accuracy of all facts and quotations as cited in this book.

Unless otherwise indicated, Bible texts are from the *Holy Bible, New International Version.* Copyright © 1973, 1978, 1984, International Bible Society. Used by permission of Zondervan Bible Publishers.
Scripture quotations credited to ESV are from *The Holy Bible,* English Standard Version, copyright © 2001 by Crossway Bibles, a division of Good News Publishers. Used by permission. All rights reserved.

This book was
Edited by Gerald Wheeler
Copyedited by James Cavil
Cover designed by Trent Truman
Cover art by iStock Photo
Electronic makeup by Shirley M. Bolivar
Typeset: Bembo 11/13

PRINTED IN U.S.A.
11 10 09 08 07   5 4 3 2 1

Library of Congress Cataloging-in-Publication Data

Tucker, Mike (Michael Duane)
   Every good thing : satisfying your hunger for God / Mike Tucker.
      p. cm.
   ISBN 978-0-8127-0449-5
   1. Christian life—Biblical teaching.   2. Bible. O.T. Psalms—Criticism, interpretation, etc.   I. Title.
   BS1430.6.C43T83 2007
   248.4—dc22

                                          2006103322

ACKNOWLEDGMENTS

Books are best when they represent a cooperative effort. Such is the case with this one. If these pages have anything of lasting value, it is because of the loving support of a community of believers. I would like to take just a few lines to acknowledge those whose belief in the project, prayers for the author, and help in every aspect of the process have made this book a possibility.

First, I would like to thank Dr. Judy Wilson, a dear friend and parishioner, for her editorial work. Dr. Wilson's careful reading of the manuscript helped catch typographical and grammatical errors.

Thanks are also due to the pastoral staff at the Arlington Seventh-day Adventist Church in Arlington, Texas, who lovingly carried the work of the church forward while the senior pastor labored over these pages. Thank you, Ion Groza, Greg Batla, Ritchie Pruehs, Kevin Wells, and Gayle Tucker. You are a great pastoral team!

The entire congregation of the Arlington Seventh-day Adventist Church should also receive thanks for allowing their senior pastor to work on many projects that fall outside the realm of normal pastoral ministry. Your prayers and loving support mean more to me than you will ever know. I praise God often for you and for your acceptance of His grace in your lives.

The staff from Faith for Today television ministries has been a wonderful support for me during the months this project took shape. Thank you for believing in our mission of carrying the gospel to everyone on the planet who views our broadcasts.

Thanks to my daughter, Allison, for her work of transcription. I know it was slow, painstaking work, but your attention to detail was a great help.

Special thanks goes to my wife, Gayle. Not only are you a wonderful pastor, but your loving support as my partner in life, the mother of my children, and colaborer on the Faith for Today broadcasts have been invaluable to me. Thank you for sharing a passion for the gospel. Thank you for not complaining when I have been gone for extended periods of time on speaking tours. Thank you for your tireless hours of labor for our Master. And thank you for loving me.

Finally, thank You, Jesus, my Lord and Savior. This book is a labor of love for You. Thank You for allowing me to experience a life of intimacy with You. Thank You for saving me. And thank You in advance for using this book to Your glory!

CONTENTS

Other books by Mike Tucker

Journal of a Lonely God
Jesus, He's All You'll Ever Need

To order, **call 1-800-765-6955.**

Visit us at **www.reviewandherald.com** for information on other
Review and Herald® products.

INTRODUCTION

U nlike much of the world, I've never experienced real hunger. I've encountered the kind that comes from missing a meal or two, but not that resulting from extended periods without food. Yet much of the world's population goes to bed hungry every night. Millions live daily without enough to eat. Starvation is a constant reality for many today, but not for me.

As I've said, I've never known that kind of physical hunger. My next meal has never seriously been in doubt. If anything, I am guilty of excess. Too often I've eaten too much or too much of the wrong kinds, but I've never truly gone without food. I cannot say that I understand the gnawing ache of physical hunger.

Spiritual hunger, however, is a different story. Its ache is very familiar to me. I know what it is like to live without the nutrients of spiritual food, without the sustenance of daily communion with God. And I know what it is like never to have feasted on the bounty of God's table.

I grew up in a religious home. We went to church every week and received a diet of the teachings of my church. My parents and church-related religious instructors were sincere in their attempts to provide a healthy religious cuisine for me. I learned how to cite proof texts in defense of doctrines. In addition, I dutifully memorized and followed a menu of prohibitions. My instruction in religion was thorough and well-intentioned. They fed me what they felt was best because they loved me and wanted me to experience spiritual growth.

However, my spiritual diet had serious deficiencies. It excluded the most important spiritual nutrients, not in an attempt to harm me, but simply because those who fed me were unaware of the existence of healthier spiritual food. Spiritual malnutrition resulted.

For years I felt an emptiness that I could not explain. My table was full of religious fare, but at the end of the day I was still hungry, longing for something more, something better. Although I ate as much and as often as I could, I was literally starving to death. An incomplete menu had left me without the most basic nutrients of the spiritual life.

Although the story of how things changed for me is too long to tell here, God was able to show me that my cravings were not for more of religion, but for the Bread of Life. My soul longed to feast on the flesh and blood of Jesus. I was hungry for God.

Only daily relationship with Him will ever satisfy our soul's hunger. Intimacy with our Redeemer is the only diet that can satisfy God hunger.

But intimacy with an unseen God is no easy task. How does one form a relationship with a Being that you cannot see, touch, or hear?

Please understand that I am not wise enough to answer these questions, but I have found those who have been able to instruct me in daily regimens that properly feed the soul. Ancient worshippers of our unseen God have left behind a journal of their religious lives with instructions as to how we can obtain that for which our souls long—genuine intimacy with God.

I am referring to the daily habits of the spiritual life, also known as the spiritual disciplines. Such ancient practices serve as aids for our growth in Christ. They are not in themselves measures of spirituality, but methods and channels for spiritual growth. Only two measurements of spiritual growth exist. We are to ask ourselves just two questions in order to determine whether we are growing in Christ. First: "Do I love Jesus more today than I did yesterday?" And second: "Do I love other human beings more today than I did yesterday?" When we are able to answer both in the affirmative, we know that we are experiencing spiritual growth.

One of the best places to learn about spiritual habits is in the Psalms. David and their other writers become our instructors. In a way they serve as our spiritual dietitians, teaching us how to eat proper spiritual food in order to receive all the essential spiritual vitamins, minerals, and nutrients necessary for growth in Christ.

A. W. Tozer wrote: "To know God is at once the easiest and the most difficult thing in the world. It is easy because the knowledge is not won by hard mental toil, but is something freely given. As sunlight falls free on the open field, so the knowledge of the holy God is a free gift to men who are open to receive it. But this knowledge is difficult because there are conditions to be met and the obstinate nature of fallen man does not take kindly to them."

Tozer then lists six conditions that we must meet in order to truly know God. They include: forsake sin; commit the whole life to Christ in faith; decide to die to sin and to be alive to God in Christ Jesus as we receive the inflowing of the Holy Spirit; repudiate the cheap values of our fallen world and separate ourselves from everything that unbelievers set their hearts upon; practice the art of long and loving meditation upon the majesty of God; and finally, make service to our fellow human beings an imperative.

As we meet these conditions and begin to develop spiritual habits, our knowledge of and intimacy with God will increase. This is the way to answer the heart's longing for Him.

This book is dedicated to viewing spiritual habits from the perspective and experience of the authors of the Psalms. At the end of each chapter I have included some suggested exercises. They are by no means exhaustive. The reader should do further study to learn more of how to employ each of the spiritual habits in daily life. It has been my purpose to provide only a primer. This book is but an introduction to the process of spiritual formation.

It is my fervent prayer that the living God will satisfy your soul's hunger. We do not need to suffer spiritual malnutrition. God has set a feast of all that we need. He has provided His flesh and blood—He has given us *Himself*. When Jesus alone is our food and our drink, we will have our souls' longings fulfilled.

CHAPTER 1

Recognize the Hunger

(Psalms 42; 43)

Researchers have announced the discovery of what some have called "the spirituality gene." Dean H. Hamer, a behavioral geneticist at the National Institutes of Health and the National Cancer Institute, has written a book entitled *The God Gene: How Faith Is Hardwired Into Our Genes.* Hamer says that spirituality is built into our genetic code. In an interview with the Washington *Post* he said: "We think that all human beings have an innate capacity for spirituality and that that desire to reach out beyond oneself, which is at the heart of spirituality, is part of the human makeup." "The research suggests some people have a bit more of that capacity than others, but it's present to some degree in everybody."

The gene that Hamer identified scientists have named VMAT2 and dubbed "the God gene." It controls the flow to the brain of chemicals that play a key role in emotions and consciousness. Hamer suggests that there are probably dozens or even hundreds more genes involved in the universal drive to seek transcendence. He further indicates that since spirituality is inherent in our genetic makeup, we cannot rid ourselves of the genetic propensity to be spiritual.

If Hamer's work proves to be true, it tells us that we were designed for fellowship with God. The Creator built a longing for intimacy with Him right into our genetic code.

Steven Curtis Chapman commented that "I really believe relationships are the greatest gifts God has given us. First and foremost, of course, is our relationship with Him. It's the reason we live and breathe, and it's the ultimate purpose of why we're here."

I remember as a boy how I would watch old movies on television. A number of them had a scene in which an actress or dancer would receive a dozen roses after her performance. The card always bore the notation "secret admirer." The movie would then depict the woman's search to discover the person's identity. Finally she would learn who the secret admirer was, and eventually they would fall in love, get married, and live happily ever after.

Our lives and our longings are a lot like those old movies. As long as we can remember, we have been hungry to know the identity of our Secret Admirer, this God who made us. And so we search to satisfy our hunger for Him—a hunger that only fellowship with Him will ever meet.

The Psalms indicate that we have a longing for God built into our very beings. In particular, Psalm 42 suggests that this is true.

Psalm 42:1, 2

"As the deer pants for streams of water, so my soul pants for you, O God. My soul thirsts for God, for the living God. When can I go and meet with God?"

Long before the work of geneticists, human beings recognized that deep within our souls we long for fellowship with God. The author of this psalm describes it as thirst. The biblical image depicts a deer in an arid land that craves water on a hot summer day. The sun beats down on its back. Its mouth is dry, and its body yearns for water above all else. The animal finds itself breathing heavily—panting, if you will—for water.

The words of this psalm tell us that our longing for God is embedded deep inside—residing in a place called the soul. Our soul thirsts for God.

If it is true that our souls hunger and thirst for God, and if it is also true that God longs for us, what keeps us apart? What keeps us from coming closer to Him and satisfying our deep craving? And what do we do in order to find God in the first place? How can we draw nearer to Him and find the intimacy our souls long for?

Perhaps the best place to discover answers to such questions is in the Psalms. It is here that we will learn how to satisfy our soul's hunger.

Most of the psalms were written as songs or prayers for worship. They are perhaps our best textbook on worship and prayer. As such, they also serve as our best guide to how to satisfy our longings for fellowship with God. If we are truly designed for intimacy with Him, the psalms will tell us how to experience that intimacy.

But where do we begin in our effort to satisfy our appetite for God? I have chosen to begin with Psalms 42 and 43 because of their vivid portrayal of our innate desire for Him. Perhaps here is where we must begin—by admitting that we have "God hunger." Let's look again at verses 1 and 2 of Psalm 42.

Verses 1, 2
"For the director of music. A maskil of the Sons of Korah. As the deer pants for streams of water, so my soul pants for you, O God. My soul thirsts for God, for the living God. When can I go and meet with God?"

Scripture attributes the psalm to "the Sons of Korah." The Korahites were Levites. Levi was the Israelite tribe dedicated to caring for the Temple. Among other things, they were the priests and Temple musicians. The Korahites belonged to the tribe of Levi and were descended through Kohath, Korah's grandfather.

When the Israelites wandered in the desert, Korah led a rebellion against Moses. He convinced 250 leaders of Israel to move against their national leader. However, God's judgment destroyed the rebels, including Korah. Korah's sons were not involved in the rebellion, and later received positions as Temple musicians. In gratitude to God for His mercy, they produced and performed music of praise to Him. One or more of Korah's descendants wrote this psalm.

The language is very descriptive, and employs a form of Hebrew poetry called parallelism. Parallelism is a literary technique involving repetition. The author presents the same thing in two or more different ways. In verse 1 the author says, "As the deer pants for streams of water" and in verse 2 he states that "my soul thirsts for God." While the two verses say the same thing, they do so in a poetical way. The psalmist describes that which is written into our genetic code—he tells of our hunger and thirst for God. He asks, "When can I go and meet with God?"

Throughout the Bible God uses many different names to depict Himself. The word used in this passage is *Elohim*. A loose translation of *Elohim* might be "mighty covenant-maker." It refers to a holy, transcendent, sovereign God who makes and keeps promises to His people. And the promise He has given is that He will be our God and that we will be His people. He has vowed a relationship of intimacy with all who seek Him. In order to ensure that we would search for Him, He built a longing for fellowship with Him right into our genetic makeup. We are built for intimacy with God.

Evidently the writer of this psalm was a lot like us. He didn't always seek God. At times he attempted to resist his spiritual genetic makeup and wandered away from God. "When can I go and meet with God?" suggests that he was not at the Temple during the time of his spiritual thirst. The Temple was where people of his time went to meet with God every day, and especially on the Sabbath.

We don't know much about the psalm's historical setting. It is possible that it was written during a time of captivity and that the sons of Korah had been exiled from the Temple. If so, we find one of the things that tend to keep us from satisfying our hunger for God. The verses indicate that a failure to worship God prevents us from fulfilling our hunger for Him. This could be a forced failure, as perhaps was the case for the psalmist, or it could be because of our own choices. Whatever the case, any attempt to deny our innate desire to worship God results in unsatisfied spiritual hunger.

In this case the cure would be to return to a worship of God—to actively seek His face through acts of worship. However, don't expect that worship alone will satisfy our longings. Eugene H. Peterson wrote: "Worship does not satisfy our hunger for God; it whets our appetite." But it is the closest we can come today to face-to-face fellowship with Him. Worship is the tool that God has given us to hold us over until we actually stand in His presence.

The psalmist tells us still other reasons that create distance between us and God.

Verses 3, 10

"My tears have been my food day and night, while men say to me all day long, 'Where is your God?'" (verse 3).

"My bones suffer mortal agony as my foes taunt me, saying to me all day long, 'Where is your God?'" (verse 10).

Sometimes the taunts of unbelievers can separate us from God. Some will abuse us for our belief in Him. They may not accept His existence, or if they do, they have so turned from Him that they will taunt us as "holier than thou" because of our faith. When it happens during the dark periods of our lives, during times of grief, unemployment, or other tragedy, it can leave us in a state of depression. We may even echo their question in our own hearts: "Where is God now?"

Do you remember watching that old movie *The Ten Commandments,* starring Charlton Heston? When the Egyptians appeared to have Moses and the Israelites trapped at the Red Sea, Edward G. Robinson, who played an antagonist in the movie, snarled, "Where's your messiah now?"

For some of us that exchange is no movie script—it's real life. And the pressure tends to leave us hungry—hungry for God, but feeling distant from Him. When life is difficult and others taunt us in the midst of our pain, we almost always feel apart from God. But even in the darkness of that hour, He longs for intimacy with us. He wants to quench our thirst— to satisfy our hunger for Him, if we will but allow Him.

A. W. Tozer wrote: "If we yearned after God even as much as a cow yearns for her calf, we would be the worshiping and effective believers God wants us to be. If we longed for God as a bride looks forward to the return of her husband, we would be a far greater force for God than we are now."

But something tends to separate us from God, and that means we are unable to satisfy our hunger for Him. The causes of separation are many, but Psalms 42 and 43 list a few. So far we have found that both failure to worship God and the taunts of unbelievers can leave us spiritually starving. Verse 4 of Psalm 42 reveals another problem that can cut us off from Him.

Verse 4

"These things I remember as I pour out my soul: how I used to go with the multitude, leading the procession to the house of God, with shouts of joy and thanksgiving among the festive throng."

Memories of better days can leave us feeling distant from God. It is a longing for "the good old days," when we knew He was close. The psalmist remembered how he used to lead the worship in the Temple. He longed to repeat those days and was so fixated on the past that it prevented him from dwelling in the here and now.

Living in the past can be disastrous. I knew a man whose wife died. In his grief he continued to live in the past to the extent that he began to exaggerate just how good it had been to be married to his now-deceased wife. Years later he found a wonderful woman and remarried. However, he was so consumed with the past that he failed to recognize what life could be like with his new wife. Eventually he drove her away and missed out on a marriage that could have been as good as, or perhaps even better than, his first one.

Yesterday may have been wonderful, but don't compare today with yesterday. Use the blessings you received yesterday as God's promise that something just as good can come your way today and tomorrow.

Verse 7

"Deep calls to deep in the roar of your waterfalls; all your waves and breakers have swept over me."

Scripture often uses the imagery of tumultuous water to represent human strife. The psalmist is saying that life's overwhelming trials tend to prevent us from satisfying our appetite for God. Trials can include such things as unemployment, grief over the loss of a loved one, marital strife, financial difficulties, problems with children, physical sickness, and a host of other things. If we are suffering through even one such event, we can feel as though a great tidal wave has swept over our life. We may fear that our present difficulty or difficulties will destroy us. At such times we feel as if God's face is hidden from us. But that's not all that separates us from Him.

Verse 9

"I say to God my Rock, 'Why have you forgotten me? Why must I go about mourning, oppressed by the enemy?'"

God's failure to act quickly on our behalf is another thing that tends to hinder intimacy with Him. All of us have had times that we have felt that He must have forgotten about us. Many who endured the Holocaust lost faith in God because of His delay in freeing those who pleaded to Him for help. I have seen people struggle with a disease or a bad marriage and become angry that God does not answer when they think He should. It feels as though He has forgotten them. Sometimes we allow such experiences to separate us from Him. One more reason for our failure to know God intimately appears in the next psalm.

Psalm 43:1

"Vindicate me, O God, and plead my cause against an ungodly nation; rescue me from deceitful and wicked men."

Attacks from ungodly, deceitful, and wicked people can make us feel distant from God. When the wicked prosper and the righteous suffer, we question His concern for us. Often those who devote themselves to God come under unjust accusation and attack. Psalms 42 and 43 list six things that tend to separate us from Him and prevent us from satisfying our hunger for Him. The list, however, is not exhaustive. But rather than focus on the problem, let's look to the solution. How do we overcome such difficulties in order to draw near to God and satisfy our soul's hunger?

First, the psalmist does not give up, but chooses to wrestle through the difficulties.

Verse 5
"Why are you downcast, O my soul? Why so disturbed within me?"

The psalmist asks himself, "What business do I have feeling sorry for myself?" The implied answer is "None." He takes himself in hand and chooses not to give in to the difficulties that he faces. As a result, he chooses positive action instead of a passive state of mind. The psalmist refuses to view himself as a victim, choosing rather to respond as a victorious child of God. But that's not all he does.

Verse 5
"Put your hope in God . . ."

Here the psalmist, by placing his hope in the Lord and rejecting a negative, passive mind-set, challenges himself to combat the things that separate him from God. But there is more.

Verses 5
". . . for I will yet praise him, my Savior and my God."

The biblical writer reminds himself that hope in God leads to praising Him. In spite of his circumstances, the psalmist chooses to proclaim God as his Savior. Whether he is in the valley around the Jordan River or on the mountain heights of Mount Hermon or Mount Mizar, he will offer his praise to God. He will worship God in spite of how he feels.

It is important to remind ourselves that just as God has led us to wonderful victories in the past, so will He do it again. Instead of focusing on what we have lost, we look instead to a positive future with our God, who is our mighty covenant keeper. What is the result of taking these three steps? We will declare with the psalmist:

Verse 2
"You are God my stronghold."

The psalmist ends by finding his confidence in God. He begins to satisfy his hunger by feeding on God through an intimate relationship with Him. So full is his recovery that he ends Psalm 43 in triumph.

Verses 3–5
"Send forth your light and your truth, let them guide me; let them bring me to your holy mountain, to the place where you dwell. Then will I go to the altar of God, to God, my joy and my

delight. I will praise you with the harp, O God, my God. Why are you downcast, O my soul? Why so disturbed within me? Put your hope in God, for I will yet praise him, my Savior and my God."

Sometimes we curse the things we think are preventing us from satisfying our hunger for God when in reality they may be what actually makes us aware that we are hungry for Him. While God does not send such difficulties, He may allow them to come in order that we will long for something more—something better. And then, when we seek Him, His love surrounds us and makes us whole.

Elizabeth was a woman with an appetite for something more. Her childhood had been an absolute nightmare. Her father was oppressive, dictatorial, and controlling. His angry rages sapped her of her strength, leaving her as a sickly, frail child who frequently had to remain confined to her bed for long periods of time.

She and her 10 siblings grew up in a living hell on earth. Elizabeth endured it in her father's house until she was nearly 40 years old. It was then that she met a wonderful man named Robert. He did not see her as a sickly middle-aged invalid but rather as a beautiful, talented spirit waiting to blossom. Loving her with all of his heart, he asked her to be his wife.

Because she had been disappointed so many times in her life, Elizabeth was afraid to trust his love. But her hunger for something more gave her the courage to trust Robert and to accept his proposal of marriage. Elizabeth's father, however, refused to allow his 40-year-old daughter to leave his home. Robert had several brutal confrontations with the man. Eventually he relented, and the couple married.

Robert and Elizabeth's love for each other was the stuff of storybooks. They traveled Europe together, enjoying fully the wonders of God's world. Their love transformed Elizabeth into the beautiful, special person her husband knew she was. At 43 she bore her husband a healthy child. Robert's love for Elizabeth was so rich that it enabled her to write beautiful sonnets of love.

Wondering if her husband would like them, one morning she quietly slipped downstairs to where he was eating breakfast, and slipped the sonnets in the pocket of his dressing gown. Robert removed them and read words that have spoken to the hearts of millions through the years. Buried in those beautiful sonnets is the immortal: "How do I love thee? Let me count the ways." Elizabeth Barrett Browning thirsted for something more. A loving relationship of deep intimacy quenched that thirst.

The same is true for each one of us. We hunger for something more.

Only intimacy with God will satisfy it. Each of us must determine today that we will not rest until we have found the One who will quench the longings of our hungry souls.

EXERCISES:

Christian author A. W. Tozer declared, "What comes into our minds when we think about God is the most important thing about us." I believe that even our longings for God are shaped by our thoughts about Him. As long as we view God as anything other than He actually is, we tend to deny that our inner cravings are for Him. It is only as we learn to think rightly about God that the awareness of our hunger for Him grows.

❖ What comes to your mind when you think about God? Are your thoughts shaped by Scripture?
❖ Read the following passages slowly. As you do so, make a list of the attributes of God you find in each passage. Once you have compiled your list, read it several times, pausing to reflect on each attribute.
  • Exodus 34:5-7
  • 2 Chronicles 2:5, 6
  • Psalm 145:8, 9
  • Psalm 147:3-9
  • Malachi 3:6
  • Mark 10:27
  • James 1:17
  • 1 John 4:8
❖ As you think about the list you prepared from the above texts, consider how God's attributes contrast with your own character. Which of God's attributes do you need most?
❖ Find a place that is comfortable and quiet. Allow yourself to imagine yourself in the story of Bartimaeus as told in Mark 10:46-52. Read the story slowly and see yourself as the person who needs something from Jesus. Picture yourself crying out to Him for help. Imagine Jesus turning to you and asking what you need. How do you answer? What need do you first express to Him? What are your greatest needs? What are your longings?
❖ Pray that God will satisfy your longings for more of Him. And pray that you will be able to allow Him to fix the areas of need in your life.

CHAPTER 2

Assurance

(Psalm 23)

Intimacy with an invisible God is not an easy thing to achieve. In fact, even intimacy with human beings, whom we can see, touch, and hear, is itself difficult, much less seeking it with an all-powerful, all-knowing, holy, transcendent, unseen deity! How do we know that He is even interested in such a relationship? Could He rebuff or ignore our overtures at closeness? Could our holy God reject us?

Insecurity filled my early teenage years. I feared rejection more than anything. My fear of rejection probably unconsciously increased the possibilities that I would be rejected.

When I turned 13, I was a little more than five feet tall and weighed about 90 pounds, a problem I can only dream about today. I had never played any organized sports and was awkward on the athletic field. My size was a real handicap in sports as well, since larger boys tended to run over my rather diminutive frame. To make matters worse, I was bookish, wore black horn-rimmed glasses, made straight A's in school, was painfully shy around girls, and had a reputation as a Goody Two-shoes. Thus I was not exactly a prime candidate for a Mr. Popularity award.

I longed to be accepted by my peers. Although I had a group of friends, not many of them were girls. I was not nearly "cool" enough to attract their attention. Besides, what self-respecting girl wanted to hang out with a guy who was small enough to be her bratty kid brother?

Eventually I grew to a more normal size for my age, but those painful years of insecurity and rejection were difficult to overcome. Even after my size was no longer an issue, asking a girl to go on a date with me was an ex-cruciating experience, since the very worst response I could possibly imagine was a giggled "No way!" As of this writing I have been happily married for nearly 30 years and would never willingly return to a life of dating. I simply have too many nightmarish memories of early teenage rejections.

Early in my attempts to approach God for a relationship of intimacy, I revisited the feelings of uncertainty I experienced as a 13-year-old boy. What if God rejected me? What if, when I asked Him to be my closest companion, He mockingly giggled, "No way"? Worse yet, what if God, who knows my every sin, evaluated my life and sneered, "What makes you think that someone as holy as I would ever want to be seen with a sinful creep like you?"

A significant part of my ministry today includes relationship counseling. I have observed that one of the greatest barriers to intimacy in relationships is the fear of rejection. Our feelings of inferiority and worthlessness cause us to set ourselves up for rejection. We tend to bring on ourselves the very thing we fear most!

God understands our fears, and I believe He has done everything He can to reassure us of His unconditional acceptance. The Lord knows that we will never attain intimacy with Him as long as we worry that He will spurn us as inferior or sinful. He realizes that where there is fear, there can never be assurance, acceptance, or even love.

1 John 4:18
"There is no fear in love. But perfect love drives out fear, because fear has to do with punishment. The one who fears is not made perfect in love."

But God offers to change all that for us. He volunteers to take away our sins so that nothing could possibly cause Him to reject us. That is why He beckons:

Isaiah 1:18
"Come now, let us reason together. . . . Though your sins are like scarlet, they shall be as white as snow; though they are red as crimson, they shall be like wool."

God reassures us that it is not in His nature to reject us.

Hebrews 13:5
"Never will I leave you; never will I forsake you."

Jesus comforts us with His love when He declares:

John 14:18

"I will not leave you as orphans; I will come to you."

Scripture constantly reminds us of God's faithfulness to us, even though He knows we are sinners. Where did we get the idea that He was eager to reject us? How did we come to the place where we felt it was our job to convince Him that He should love us and accept us?

I believe Satan's greatest triumph has been to distort our understanding of God's character. He has led us to believe things about the Lord that are not true. Jesus said that when He is lifted up so that all can see Him exactly as He is, He will then draw everyone to Himself. Why? Because when we get a glimpse of the true character of the Godhead, we will find it irresistible! We lose our fear of rejection and luxuriate in the opulence of acceptance.

So who is God? What is He really like? How does He relate to us?

One of the places in Scripture that we find answers to such questions is in a familiar psalm. It is one of the world's favorite psalms, and often gets recited at funerals, although it was not written to be a funerary psalm.

People frequently refer to Psalm 23 as the Shepherd's Psalm or the Shepherd's Prayer. As I have studied this psalm, I find in it a picture of God that is simply irresistible. As we take a closer look at this psalm, see if you don't agree.

We noted already that the psalms were written as songs and as prayers. If this psalm is a prayer, then we find seven petitions in it. The first is "Lord, be my God," and it appears in verse 1.

Psalm 23:1

"The Lord is my shepherd, I shall not be in want."

The first five words alone form a wonderful prayer. What those words imply is so deep, and so rich, and so meaningful that it alone would be enough of a prayer for anyone.

Scripture calls God by many names, each with its own special meaning. The name used here is the same one that we find in Exodus 3. As Moses stood before the burning bush, it spoke to him and said, "I want you to do something for Me. I want you to go to the children of Israel." Moses replied, "If I go, whom should I say sent me?" God then gave Moses a name for Himself that appears some 4,000 times elsewhere in the Bible. We could translate it as I AM WHO I AM.

That name tells us that God is all-sufficient. He doesn't depend on anyone else. Nor does He need anything from you or me. Although our church may call for our tithes and offerings, God doesn't need them. We need to give them because it is an act of worship and an indication of our dependence upon Him. He doesn't really need anything from us—our worship, our praise, or our service. Able to do anything He wants to do without us, He is completely and totally self-sufficient.

As we look at this self-sufficient and sovereign God, we see ourselves in contrast to Him. What we find is that we are very needy, requiring Him for our next breath, for our next word, for our next thought. We need Him if we are to do anything of any value, because we are totally and completely dependent upon our holy God. He is sovereign, and we are not. He is exulted above all others, and we are nothing, because He is "the Lord."

As we struggle to get our minds to comprehend all that, we find that Scripture also calls our all-sufficient, exalted, and sovereign Lord a shepherd.

Almost every culture of the world ranks that occupation at the very bottom rung of the social ladder. It was so low that in families with several sons, the youngest son always got the dirty job of caring for the sheep.

Ancient Israel often did not allow shepherds to enter the Temple complex or to participate in worship since their job required them to perform tasks that left them ceremonially unclean. They had to go through a period of cleansing before they could pray in the Temple.

The relationship between shepherd and sheep was extremely close. Not only did the sheep depend upon the shepherd for every aspect of life, but the shepherd depended on the sheep as well. The sheep represented the shepherd's livelihood. In the days before a public welfare system or Social Security, if the sheep perished, the shepherd would starve. If the shepherd owned the sheep, he was willing to die for them, because they were the family business and, therefore, the family income.

Caring for sheep was a 24-hour-a-day job because sheep are basically helpless. Very stupid animals, they don't know enough to come in out of the rain. They have no means of protecting themselves, have poor eyesight, and aren't fast enough to run away from their enemies. Sheep need help with every detail of life. So a shepherd had to be with them 24 hours a day, seven days a week. The shepherd had to sleep out in the fields with the flock in both good weather and bad. The shepherd was always on duty in one of the worst jobs possible.

As human beings we need a shepherd because we're a whole lot like sheep. In many ways we're too dumb to come in or go out. We are unable to survive in a sinful world. But the incredible news is that the exulted

God has offered to be our Shepherd. The "I AM WHO I AM" promises to care for His helpless sheep.

Verse 1

"I shall not be in want."

God supplies all our needs. But what are they? David outlines them in the six requests of his psalm. The first request is simply "Be my God, Lord." He asks for the great God of the universe to be his Lord and shepherd—to be the "I AM WHO I AM" for him.

The second petition of this prayer is "Lord, give me rest," and appears in verse 2.

Verse 2

"He makes me lie down in green pastures, he leads me beside quiet waters."

I have not had much dealing with sheep, but I am told that it is very difficult to get them to lie down. Four things must not be present, or they will refuse to rest. The first thing that has to be missing is fear. If sheep are afraid, they will not lie down. As long as they sense some threat, they will refuse to relax.

The next thing that must be gone is insect pests. Ticks, lice, and especially flies will bother sheep. Sheep must be free of parasites if they are to find rest.

The third thing that will prevent sheep from lying down is friction or hostility between the animals. Sheep cannot be at odds with other sheep if they are to get any rest. If there is any animosity with other sheep, they're going to stand their ground. However, when the sheep are getting along with each other and everything is peaceful, then they will let their guard down and make themselves comfortable.

The last thing that must not be there is famine. When sheep rest in green pastures, they are lying down in their food. Sheep must have an abundance of food, or they will be worried about where their next meal is coming from. The flock must feel full. Only then will they lie down and find rest.

I find the same things to be true of people. If we are afraid, we get no rest. Do you find yourself awake in bed at night worrying about what might happen? Does fear prevent you from attempting to do something great for God? Jesus tells us that He has not given us a "spirit of fear" (2 Tim. 1:7, KJV). Fear is the enemy of our faith. Place your trust in Jesus and allow Him to give each one of us peace.

Parasites such as bad habits or injurious sins can prevent us from finding rest. When friction with other members of the church or anyone in the community or home exists, there will be no rest for us. Outsiders will notice the tensions and will steer clear of such a group. Why would they want to be a part of something that is embroiled in an internal fight? A congregation struggling with friction is a church that will not grow, and a believer with friction in life is a believer who will find no rest.

If we are fearful about a lack of food—if we are not spiritually or physically fed—we will have no rest. We cannot experience a famine of God's Word and not expect to be weak and worried. Do you read Scripture as a book of proof texts, or have you learned to move beyond the infant's milk we offer to new believers? Have you discovered how to mine the Word as a rich storehouse of spiritual food that enables genuine growth in the knowledge and presence of God?

Isn't it interesting that this psalm begins with rest? Right after David asks the Lord to be his God, he asks Him for rest. This should not surprise us. God created Adam and Eve on a Friday. In fact, the day was already well in progress. So the very first full day of existence for them was Saturday, the Sabbath. So the first couple actually began their existence with a full day of rest. God said, "You know, being created was work enough for you. It's time to take a nap. It's time to rest." His concern for humanity's limitations is so great that He makes provision for us and gives us rest. David asked God to give him rest, and so should we.

Psalm 23:3
"He restores my soul."

"God, grant me life and health," the psalmist petitions. Has your soul ever needed such restoration?

We could interpret the passage in two different ways. It could mean either that David is talking about the restoration brought about through repentance and salvation, or that he has in mind the gift of physical health and life. Neither interpretation does violence to the passage, but I think that the major emphasis is on the latter.

Have you been physically healed? People in my congregation have experienced it. For some God took away chronic pain. In others He removed cancer. I've also seen Him repair damaged relationships. But we must always keep in mind that He doesn't do it every time we ask. He is God and we are not, so we must trust Him to heal physically, relationally, and spiritually when it is best to do so. Yet it is exciting to witness the times God does choose to heal His people. He truly restores our souls.

In the church I pastor, at least three or four times a year we dedicate our prayer meeting to healing. We announce that we are going to hold a healing service and invite anyone in need of physical, relational, spiritual, or emotional healing to come for prayer. Those with addictions and other problems receive invitations as well. As instructed in the book of James, we anoint the person with oil. All of us gather around those who request healing, and we lay hands on them and pray. Some get healed immediately; others are healed over time with medicine, therapy, or even surgery; and still others will receive their healing on resurrection morning. God answers every prayer for healing in the affirmative. He cures our diseases.

At times it seems that everything in life has turned upside done. During such periods we especially need restoration.

Phillip Keller tells us that when sheep rest in the green grass, they might unknowingly lie beside a depression in the ground. If the sheep rolls back just a bit, its weight might cause it to slide or flip over into the sunken spot. The sheep then finds itself caught with its legs in the air. Since a sheep's body is thick and heavy, especially when its coat of wool is heavy, and the legs are skinny and light, it is almost impossible for a sheep in such a predicament to right itself. Shepherds call an animal in such a predicament a "cast sheep."

Sheep usually panic when that happens. They begin to kick and flail away in a desperate effort to right themselves. All of this frantic activity can build up gasses in the body and restrict the flow of blood to the extremities. Eventually the feet grow numb. If the sheep is not turned over, it will die. A shepherd must right the sheep, hold it between his legs, and massage the limbs of the sheep to get the blood flowing again before it perishes.

This paints a picture of God's care for us. Deeply concerned about our predicament, He longs to right us when we are cast. He offers us health and healing.

In his next request David says, "Lord, please be my guide."

Psalm 23:3
"He guides me in paths of righteousness for His name's sake."
When we ask God to direct our lives, He leads us in "paths of righteousness."

During the winter shepherds in Palestine grazed their sheep in the valley. In the summer they would take them to the higher elevations. Very often, getting to the mountain plateaus involved following dangerous paths.

Shepherds in the Middle East lead their sheep, whereas those in the Western world tend to use dogs to drive their flocks. A Middle Eastern shepherd knows each animal by name. The sheep know the shepherd and recognize his voice and their name when called. And they listen to the shepherd's voice and follow it.

Jesus says that His sheep hear His voice, know His voice, and follow His voice. They confidently follow Him since He leads them only along safe paths.

The sheep trust the shepherd to know the best paths to take to get them to the high pastures so that they can safely graze. They go wherever the shepherd does.

At times people tell me, "I can't ask God for guidance. I've been so far away from Him! My life is so far removed from anything it should be, so how can I ask Him for help? I don't deserve to come into His presence and request such things."

I can answer, based on this and other passages, "You're right! You don't deserve it. Not a person on earth does. But it doesn't matter how far away from God you have wandered. He can hear your voice and is willing to help you anyway."

Notice what the psalmist says about why God leads undeserving sheep. David says, "He guides me in paths of righteousness for *his name's sake.*"

You see, it's not about you. It's always about Him. When we come to believe that we have drifted too far from God for Him to answer when we pray, we have fallen into the trap of egocentricity. We have become the center of our universe. But if God is the center of our universe—if our perspective is theocentric rather than egocentric—then it does not matter how far we have wandered away. All that matters is how strong, how willing, and how gracious our loving God is toward His wayward sheep. It is not because they deserve it, but because He deserves to do it. God guides us because He has promised to do exactly that. As a result, He must be true to Himself—to His own character, His attributes—and that means that He will guide every undeserving sheep who calls on His name. Thus He helps us for His name's sake, not for our sake.

This is wonderful news. If I depend upon what I deserve, I'm in real trouble. But if I depend upon that which God deserves, then I'm in great shape! God alone is worthy, and that is the basis of His choice to guide unworthy sheep.

Some may fear that they have fallen so far that God could never bless them—that they are too sinful for Him to save. But every time any of us feel that way, we have been victimized by a lie. The lie is that it is all about us. But as we have seen, it is not all about us or about what we deserve. It always has to do with God and who He is, and what He deserves.

Even at our best, we are not worthy enough for what God has promised to do for us. Isaiah tells us that our very best righteous acts are as "filthy rags" (Isa. 64:6). Suffice it to say that our best acts of righteousness are still so polluted as to be disgusting, deserving to be thrown out with the trash. That's about the best we can muster!

Paul adds his thoughts to those of Isaiah. He declares that all of his best acts of righteousness are, as one translation calls it, "dung." Actually, Paul uses the vernacular term, a word that most Christians today would blush to hear in mixed company, much less from the pulpit as read from Scripture.

The Bible writers agree that on our own, we can offer absolutely nothing to God as evidence that even the best of us deserve to be guided by a holy God. But, praise God, it is not about us! It is about Him and who He is. He chooses to guide us "for his name's sake." And in that fact lies our security.

David's next petition is for safety. "Lord, please keep me safe."

Verse 4

"Even though I walk through the valley of the shadow of death, I will fear no evil, for you are with me."

You will remember we learned that in the summer sheep grazed on the high plateaus. Summers are great for sheep. It was cooler on the mountains in the summer, the days were longer, and fewer predators roamed the heights.

But winters were a different story. During them the shepherd took the sheep into the valley to graze. The days were shorter, and in a valley surrounded by mountains, it was darker, creating more shadows in which the more numerous predators could hide. To sheep, every valley was a "valley of the shadow of death," since death could very well lurk in the shadows. If the sheep were unaccompanied by a shepherd, the winter valleys with their reduced sunlight and increased shadows were very dangerous. Sheep wandering by themselves were easy prey.

Notice that even God's sheep walk through "the valley of the shadow of death." We don't spend all of our time in green pastures and beside quiet waters. Eventually every sheep finds itself traversing shadowy and deadly valleys. You've been there. And if you haven't yet, guess what? It's coming. You'll be there eventually. All of us will.

When we journey through the "valley of the shadow" unaccompanied by our shepherd, fear is our constant companion. Paralyzing fear causes us to wonder, *How am I going to get through this? What's going to happen to me? What's going to happen to those around me, those who depend on me?* Fear makes us dread the future.

But God's sheep have no need for fear, because He is our shepherd. He is looking out for us.

I get myself into a lot of trouble by saying yes too often. I make too many commitments. Then, when I realize that I am not able to do all the things I promised to do, a sick feeling lodges in the pit of my stomach. I begin to worry. I carry responsibility for a large congregation, a Christian school that runs from prekindergarten through grade 12, a worldwide television ministry, various speaking appointments, and deadlines for books. When I stop to think about all these things, panic threatens to overwhelm me.

But God tells me, "You've got no business worrying, Mike. First of all, it's not your church, and it's not your school, and it's not your ministry. They all belong to Me. I've asked you to do something, that's all. Let Me do the worrying. Your responsibility is just to be faithful." I struggle to remember that.

The same thing is true for our lives. Whether it's our bills, our children, our job, or our God-given ministry, He tells us to let Him do the worrying. We must just concentrate on being faithful in following the Shepherd, and He will do the rest. Woody Allen said, "Eighty percent of the success in life is showing up." That's one of the few times I agree with him. Show up. Be faithful. Do what God has called us to do and let Him worry. He's going to keep us safe. He will guide us through the valley of the shadow of death.

The next part of that verse says:

Verse 4
"Your rod and your staff, they comfort me."
Christian scholar William Barclay tells us that in Bible times a rod was a stick with a big gnarled wooden ball at the end of it. Often the shepherd would drive nails partway into the ball in order to make it a more formidable weapon. Also he would drill a small hole at the base of the handle and run a leather strap through the hole so that he could tie it to the waist sash on his clothing. The rod was a weapon of defense. If a wild an-

imal attacked, the shepherd had a club par excellence. Then he could just whale away at any animal or a robber who wanted to steal the sheep.

The staff was a long stick with a crook that served two purposes. One involved correction. If a sheep wandered too far away from the flock, the shepherd would rap it on the nose to remind it to stay closer to the rest of the sheep. The other role was rescue. If a sheep fell into a ravine, the shepherd could hook it under its front legs and haul it to safety. The shepherd would also place the hooked end of the staff around a large stone or a tree and then hold on to the straight end of the staff as he lowered himself into the ravine in order to rescue the sheep.

Protection, correction, and rescue! The shepherd provides all of those for His sheep. Because of that, we need have no fear, even when trapped in the valley of the shadow of death.

The next petition is: "Lord, please provide for me."

Verse 5
"You prepare a table before me in the presence of my enemies."

The imagery of the table makes me think about the American holiday Thanksgiving. At Thanksgiving my wife and her mother and sisters prepare more food than we can possibly consume at one sitting. They cook for two days, and when finally the food is done, they set the table with the very best tablecloth, china, and silverware. A beautiful flower arrangement decorates the table, and candles glow, making a visual experience that enhances the culinary.

After we have summoned the family to eat, but before we sit down at the table, we always have to take a photograph of the table. I've never understood the reason for it, but I do not argue. Some things are best left unquestioned. I've been married for 30 years and now have 30 photographs of tables filled with food!

But for a shepherd, preparing the table meant something quite different. Phillip Keller tells us that before a shepherd would allow his sheep to graze in a field, he would first crawl through that field on his hands and knees. The shepherd would pull up poisonous, noxious weeds, and cut back dangerous briars and thorns. He would attempt to remove anything that might harm the sheep, a practice called "preparing the table."

The shepherd might do it "in the presence of my enemies." Wild animals and thieves may lurk in the shadows, but the sheep had no fear as long as the shepherd was near.

Your enemy, the accuser of all humanity, lurks in the shadows as your Shepherd provides for you. As he watches, your Shepherd cares for your every need. He loves, accepts, and forgives you. These are your most basic needs. Yet He offers much, much more.

The psalmist adds:

Verse 5
"You anoint my head with oil."

Oil is a symbol of the Holy Spirit, a symbol of healing, and a symbol of the fat of the land. Every shepherd carried a mixture of olive oil, sulfur, and spices to promote the healing of wounds. When a sheep cut itself on some sharp stone or briar, the shepherd would wash the wound and then pour this mixture of oil and spices into it. The oil not only soothed the wound and promoted healing, but it also kept away flies and other parasites.

Oil is for healing. When the Holy Spirit, as represented by oil, enters your life, He soothes and heals your wounds. God makes provision for every area of your existence.

So completely does God provide that David declares that he has an abundant supply of everything.

Verse 5
"My cup overflows."

That means that you've got more than you need. We live in a land of plenty. At times we may feel as if we haven't anything, but if we compare ourselves to the rest of the world, we are embarrassingly wealthy. I may complain that I'm driving a Honda Civic instead of the Lexus I want, but people in some parts of the world would be thrilled to have a 15-year-old Honda Civic.

The psalm has one last petition. David asks, "Lord, please take me home."

Verse 6
"Surely goodness and love will follow me all the days of my life, and I will dwell in the house of the Lord forever."

The word translated as "love" is my favorite Hebrew word, *hesed*. *Hesed* is so rich in its meaning that it requires at least 26 English words to capture its breadth and depth. It means love, but it is love taken to a fever pitch of devotion. The lover is possessed with the beloved so much so that they can never get them off their mind. It is an intensely loyal form of love.

Scripture, especially the book of Deuteronomy, uses it to describe God's love for men and women, telling us that God is crazy about us, that He will never let us go or give up on us. Such is the strength of His love for us.

When the psalmist declares that "goodness and love" will "follow" us for the entirety of life, it means that you can never get away from God's devoted love. Today and throughout all eternity, it matters not where you go or what you do. God's *hesed* love is right there, following you. You cannot get away from it.

God doesn't love you more when you're good than when you're bad. His love for you is unchanging and never-ending. He's never been so angry about what you've done that He quit loving you. Such divine love will follow you all the days of your life.

This passage also tells us that we will dwell in God's house forever. If you grew up in a home with a father who really loved you, who nurtured you and cared for you and met your needs and encouraged you, then this means something to you. But if you didn't have such a father, this passage could trouble you. So I encourage you to imagine the father you've always wanted, the kind you wish that you'd grown up with. Stretch your imagination and make him far better than you could ever possibly wish for a father to be. Then, when you get that picture firmly planted in your mind, multiply it by a million. If you could do that, you would still fall short of the truth about how good your heavenly Father really is. It is in His house that you will dwell forever. And it is His love that will envelope you. Throughout the ceaseless ages of eternity you will live in His house and experience His love and acceptance in your life. That's the promise!

So who is God? What is He really like? How does He relate to us? Some of the best answers I've found are in Psalm 23. He is your God—the God who gives us rest, grants us health and life, guides us, keeps us safe, provides for us, and who will eventually take us home. Here is the picture that He paints of Himself.

In the days of the old west a pastor cared for a group of farmers. His parish was rather far-flung, covering a large territory.

One day he learned that the young son of a family in a rather remote part of his parish was in the last stages of life. The pastor hitched his horse and buggy and rode out to see what he could do to help the family.

When he arrived, he saw that the family had grown weary from caring for their son. Although the boy was still alert, he could no longer speak. Since the family wanted to be with him when he died, they had remained awake with the boy.

The pastor told the family to go to bed and get some rest while he cared for the boy. He promised to awaken them if the lad's condition changed. The family agreed and went to bed for some much-needed sleep.

As the pastor cared for the boy, he attempted to communicate the gospel. He wanted the boy to know that he had no reason for fear since God loved and accepted him. However, since the boy could not talk, the pastor did not know if he understood.

That evening the family awakened, and the pastor went home. Early the next morning he returned. When he arrived, the family informed him that their son had passed away that evening just a few hours after the pastor had departed. They thanked the pastor for his help, which had enabled them to be fresh and alert when their son died.

The family, however, had a question for the pastor. Shortly after he had gone, their son had taken the ring finger of his right hand and placed it firmly inside the fist of his left hand. He had held on to that finger with all his might, and died that way. The family had left him in his bed, still clutching the finger. They wondered if the pastor understood the significance of his behavior.

The pastor said he knew exactly what it meant. "I wanted your son to die without fear, so I attempted several different ways of communicating the gospel to him," the man explained. "I wanted him to know that he was loved and accepted by God, and that his salvation was certain. One of the ways I attempted to do this was through the first five words of the Shepherd's Psalm, Psalm 23.

"I took his thumb and squeezed it, saying, 'The. There is only one. He alone is God.'

"Then I squeezed his index finger and said, 'Lord. He is Lord of all things. That means that He is in charge of all things and is able to do anything that He wills. He is God.'

"Next I squeezed his middle finger and said, 'Is.' He is not just the God of yesterday and not just the God of tomorrow; He is the God of today. He is God this very minute, and He is present with us even during this dark hour.'

"Then I squeezed his ring finger and said, 'My. He belongs to you and you belong to Him, and nothing can change that. You belong to the Shepherd. You are one of His lambs, and He will not allow anyone to steal you away from His fold.'

"Finally, I took his pinkie and said, 'Shepherd. He is the Shepherd, you are the lamb, and if you will trust Him, He will carry you to His fold.'"

Then the pastor said, "I guess the word that meant the most to your son was 'my.' He knew that he belonged to the Shepherd and that the Shepherd belonged to him, and nothing could change that fact!"

EXERCISES:

❖ Pray Psalm 23 at least three times each day for a week. At the end of each prayer, thank God that He will never leave you or forsake you. Thank Him for the ways He cares for you. Learn to live daily with the assurance that you are accepted in Christ.

❖ Attempt to visualize what it must be like for God to care for your needs the way a shepherd does those of each sheep. See yourself as God's lamb.

❖ Read and memorize the following passages. Allow them to remind you that the Good Shepherd will never reject you.
  • Isaiah 1:18
  • John 14:18
  • Hebrews 13:5
  • 1 John 4:18

❖ Remembering the last story from this chapter, place the ring finger of your right hand inside your left hand and pray the following prayer.

"Lord Jesus, I need a Shepherd. Just like a lamb, I am helpless to do anything for myself. I cannot protect myself from the enemy, I cannot make right choices, and I cannot find my way without Your guidance. I confess that I am a sinner and do not deserve a shepherd like You, but I ask that You forgive my sins and accept me as Your lamb. Teach me to recognize Your voice so that I might always follow You. Make me obedient to Your every command. Help me to depend completely on You for every need and every decision of my life. I claim You as my shepherd and believe that absolutely nothing can change the fact that I belong to You and You belong to me. Thank You, Lord Jesus, for always accepting me. I rest secure in the assurance that You love me as Your own. Amen."

CHAPTER 3

Repentance

(Psalm 32)

D. L. Moody wrote that "man is born with his face turned away from God. When he truly repents, he is turned right round toward God; he leaves his old life."

It is as though our natural inclination is to run from God—to hide from Him as our first parents, Adam and Eve, did so long ago. Ever since that day we have hungered for more of God while our inclination is to flee from Him. But if we are ever to satisfy our hunger for God, we must stop trying to escape His presence and do an about-face toward Him. The first step toward God is repentance.

Bill Watterson is the cartoonist who drew *Calvin and Hobbes*. In a collection of his cartoons entitled *The Essential Calvin and Hobbes,* Calvin says to his tiger friend, Hobbes, "I feel bad that I called Susie names and hurt her feelings. I'm sorry I did it."

"Maybe you should apologize to her," Hobbes suggests.

Calvin thinks about this for a while, then replies, "I keep hoping there's a less obvious solution."

Not only is it true that we were born with our faces away from God; it is equally true that our spirit recoils at the thought of repentance. In the case of intimacy with God, the obvious solution is the correct solution. But what is repentance and how does one go about the business of repenting?

Ilion T. Jones shed some light on this question when he wrote, "Repentance is not a fatal day when tears are shed, but a fatal day when, as a result of tears, a new life begins."

Repentance is not primarily a religious word. We get the word from a nomadic culture. Its people lived in a world with no maps. Since one sand dune looks a lot like the next sand dune, it's easy to get lost walking through the desert. A traveler who suddenly decided that he or she was heading in the wrong direction would turn from the current direction and start out in a new one.

The first act of repentance is to admit that we are going in the wrong direction. Many have called the step that of confession.

The second act of repentance is to change directions. It implies an admission to others of our having followed a wrong course and our need for a new one.

A. W. Tozer summarizes: "To move across from one sort of person to another is the essence of repentance: the liar becomes truthful; the thief, honest; the lewd, pure; the proud, humble."

For an understanding of how this affects the spiritual life, we turn to King David. David wrote Psalm 32, which is a wonderful example of a prayer of repentance. Scripture labels it a *maskil,* perhaps with the idea of "the giving of instruction." In order to understand this psalm properly we must recognize its historical context. David composed it in response to his sin with Bathsheba. You remember the story of how the king remained at home while his army went to war. His generals suggested that David, who was now getting a bit older, should stay at home and allow the younger men to fight the battles so as not to risk his life.

One evening as his army was in the field, David stood on a balcony at the palace and saw Bathsheba, the wife of Uriah the Hittite, bathing in plain view. Uriah was a soldier who was fiercely loyal to David and to Israel. The king ordered that Bathsheba be brought to him, and he committed adultery with her. Upon learning that she was pregnant with his child, the king attempted to hide his sin, and eventually orchestrated a battle in such a way that it caused Uriah's death. Afterward the prophet Nathan came to David and confronted him with his sins. David admitted everything and repented. Then he wrote Psalm 51 as an immediate response to his experience of repentance.

In Psalm 51 David made a promise to God. He vowed that if the Lord would forgive and restore him, he would instruct others in the ways of God.

Psalm 51:13

"Then I will teach transgressors your ways, and sinners will turn back to you."

It appears that he wrote Psalm 32 some time later as a partial fulfillment of this promise.

REPENTANCE

Through the centuries this psalm has instructed millions, including such luminaries as the apostle Paul, who quoted the psalm in Romans 4 as support for his claim that salvation is by faith in Jesus alone. Another famous Christian it guided was Augustine, an early church leader who had it inscribed on the wall next to his bed. "The beginning of knowledge is to know oneself to be a sinner," he observed at one point. He even meditated on the psalm as he lie dying.

When one makes a thorough study of Psalm 32, it becomes apparent that we are all sinners in need of repentance. Let's look at the psalm and learn how to use the tool of repentance in order to come close to God.

Psalm 32:1, 2

"Blessed is he whose transgressions are forgiven, whose sins are covered. Blessed is the man whose sin the Lord does not count against him and in whose spirit is no deceit."

As we have already observed, psalms are religious poems that were used as songs and as prayers for both public and private worship. Again let us remind ourselves that a common feature of Hebrew poetry is parallelism—a practice of saying the same thing in at least two different ways in the same stanza of the poem. In this example of parallelism David uses three different words for sin and gives us three corresponding ways that God deals with our sin.

James Montgomery Boice explains the meanings of these three Hebrew words. The first word for sin is translated here as "transgressions." It indicates "a going away," "departure," or "a rebellion" against God and His authority. Here David employs the word to imply the idea of rebellion.

When we confess our sins, God takes the sin off our back. Psalm 103 tells us that He removes it "as far as the east is from the west." In Isaiah 43 the prophet tells us that God chooses to forget our sins—that He no longer even remembers them.

The second thing that this psalm reveals about what God does with our sin is that He covers it.

Verse 1

"Blessed is he whose transgressions are forgiven, whose sins are covered."

The imagery alludes to the Temple services on the Day of Atonement. On that day the high priest carried the blood of a goat into the Most Holy Place and sprinkled it on the ark of the covenant. The ark was a wooden box overlaid with gold. On the top of the box were two angels, or cheru-bim, who spread their wings across the ark. The space beneath their wings represented God's presence. The lid or covering of the ark, the place where the blood was sprinkled, was called the mercy seat. Underneath the mercy seat, inside the ark, rested the stone tablets inscribed with the Ten Commandments.

When the high priest sprinkled the blood over the ark on the mercy seat, it symbolized the blood of Jesus covering the broken law. It meant that the sinner had been spared from judgment. So David tells us that our "sins are covered" by the blood of Jesus, and that we are spared from pun-ishment.

The third word tells us what God does not do.

Verse 2
"Blessed is the man whose sin the Lord does not count against him."

The word "count" is a bookkeeping term. Paul, in Romans, tells us that God puts our sin into Christ's ledger as a debit, and places Christ's righ-teousness into our ledgers as a credit. What all of this means is that when we confess our sin before our God, He takes its burden and removes it from us, He covers our sin with Jesus' shed blood, and He debits Christ's account with our sin while crediting our account with the righteousness of Jesus.

Charles Colson was convicted for his participation in the Watergate break-in during the Nixon presidency. As a result, he spent time in prison. Colson, who has since confessed his guilt and found forgiveness in Christ, wrote: "Repentance is the process by which we see ourselves, day by day, as we really are: sinful, needy, dependent people. It is the process by which we see God as He is: awesome, majestic, and holy."

Repentance is not something to fear. When we confess our sins and are willing to turn away from them, we always find acceptance from God. First John 1:9 assures us that "if we confess our sins, he is faithful and just to forgive us our sins, and to cleanse us from all unrighteousness" (KJV).

A. W. Tozer observed that "deliverance can come to us only by the defeat of our old life. Safety and peace come only after we have been forced to our knees. God rescues us by breaking us, by shattering our strength and wiping out our resistance."

Confession should not terrify us, because God greets it with accep-tance and forgiveness. In fact, the cleansing power of God is the only thing that can enable us to have true repentance, a turning from sin. If you feel that you are distant from God, the first steps toward Him include confessing that you've been heading in the wrong direction. It involves asking for forgiveness for going in that direction and then rejoices in the reality of our Father's forgiveness and acceptance. Our sin is an offense to God. An act of rebellion against Him, it hurts Him more than it does anyone else.

A fine Scottish Christian was also a successful businessman. He had only one son, and he was proud of this boy. The son had a wonderful education and was highly respected in the community. But one day the authorities arrested the son for embezzlement. As his trial proceeded, the evidence against him became overwhelming. Even though his guilt was obvious to everyone, the young man was unrepentant and proud, refusing to admit that he had done anything wrong.

When the trial ended, the jury found the young man guilty. Still, he was unwilling to admit to wrongdoing, and continued to be unrepentant. When it was time for sentencing, the judge told the young man to stand for the sentence. As he did, still somewhat cocky and proud, he glanced around the courtroom. Then he noticed that over at his attorney's side his father had arisen to his feet as well. His father had recognized that he also was involved with the problem of what his boy had become.

The young man looked and saw that his father—a man who had once walked straight and tall—now stood with his shoulders bowed low with sorrow and shame as though he were about to receive the sentence from the judge. At the sight of his father, bent and humiliated, the son finally began to weep bitterly and for the first time repented of his crime.

Our sin does not affect just us—it affects our Father as well. Only our recognition of this fact can lead us to genuine sorrow for sin. I like this statement by W. M. Taylor: "True repentance hates the sin, and not merely the penalty; and it hates the sin most of all because it has discovered and felt God's love."

When we discover God's love, and when we learn how much our sin hurts the God who loves us so, it changes our attitude. No longer are we haughty and proud. Now, broken by the weight of our guilt, we abhor the evil we have done to our Father.

Verses 3-5 of our psalm describe the effect that unconfessed guilt has on our lives.

Verses 3-5
"When I kept silent, my bones wasted away through my groaning all day long. For day and night your hand was heavy

upon me; my strength was sapped as in the heat of summer. Then I acknowledged my sin to you and did not cover up my iniquity. I said, 'I will confess my transgressions to the Lord'— and you forgave the guilt of my sin."

Nothing saps the energy more than a guilty conscience. Unresolved guilt removes all joy from life. Martin Luther was one who struggled with guilt. Sometimes his guilt involved real sins, and at other times it concerned imagined sins. Whether the guilt was over real sins or not, it threatened to destroy him. He couldn't sleep because of the overwhelming feelings. They tormented him all day and all night. Before his break with the Catholic Church, he went to confession every day and was so guilt-ridden by his sins he would almost have gone every hour. On most nights Luther slept well, but he even felt guilty about that, thinking, *Here am I, sinful as I am, having a good night's sleep.* So he would confess that.

One day the older priest to whom Luther went for confession said to him, "Martin, either find a new sin and commit it, or quit coming to see me!"

But the good news is that Jesus never attacked anyone who felt guilty. He recognized their sorrow for sin and forgave them. The only people He ever condemned were the self-righteous, because He knew they could not be forgiven until they actually felt guilty.

God's judgment was heavy upon David. Depressed by day, he couldn't sleep at night. And believe it or not, this was good news! The foul odor of guilt is good news because it alerts us to the fact that something isn't right—that we need to make changes in our lives.

On March 18, 1937, a school building in New London, Texas, exploded, killing more than 300 people, most of them children. How did it happen? The local school board had wanted to cut heating costs. So they siphoned natural gas, a by-product of petroleum extraction, from a neighboring oil company's pipeline in an attempt to fuel the building's furnace free of charge. But the connections to the furnace in the basement had some leaks. Natural gas seeped out and filled the basement. A spark ignited the gas, and the rest is history.

Why didn't anyone notice that natural gas had accumulated? Because natural gas has no smell. In response to this terrible explosion, the government began requiring companies to add an odorant to natural gas. The distinctive aroma is now so familiar that we often forget natural gas has no odor itself. Today, whenever natural gas leaks, you can smell the stench and take measures to avert an explosion.

The foul smell of guilt is God's gift that helps us avoid disaster. When we notice that something is wrong, we find ourselves driven to our knees to seek the solution to our problem.

Verses 4, 5

"My strength was sapped as in the heat of summer. Then I acknowledged my sin to you and did not cover up my iniquity. I said, 'I will confess my transgressions to the Lord'—and you forgave the guilt of my sin."

First notice that when David confessed, God forgave immediately. The king didn't have to wait. Complete forgiveness came instantly. Also, verse 5 has the same words for sin contained in verses 1 and 2. Here in verse 5 we have them translated as "iniquity," "transgressions," and "sin."

The first word refers to sin as rebellion against God, the second to sin as falling short of the target that is God's law, and the third to sin as something twisted or corrupted. David uses those same words in verse 5 in order to show that he had confessed his sin completely, holding back nothing.

If I acknowledge that I did something wrong, but then go right ahead and say, "But I was really provoked by what you did to me," then I'm not really confessing. Instead, I'm rationalizing. That is not complete repentance. Complete repentance declares, "This is what I did, and I blame no one but myself. What someone else may have done to provoke me is of no consequence. I am responsible for what I did, and I am in the wrong." Now, that is true confession! It represents genuine repentance. This is what David did. And just as soon as the king repented, God forgave him completely.

Verse 5 is the longest verse in the psalm. At the end of verse 4 we find the word *selah*. It also appears at the end of verse 5. *Selah* is probably a direction to musicians, and most likely calls for a pause in the music. The pause emphasizes something of significance. Thus verse 5 begins and ends with a pause, as though David is saying, "Take notice of this. This is the most important part of the entire psalm."

When we have been forgiven, it is good to pause to consider God's goodness toward us. However, we find no pause between the words "I will confess my transgressions to the Lord" and the words "you forgave the guilt of my sin." That indicates that the forgiveness was immediate, without delay.

Doesn't this remind you of the story of the prodigal son? When the prodigal decided to go home to his father, he rehearsed a little speech of confession and repentance. But the father knew what his son intended to say before he said it. He didn't even let him get the words out before he forgave the son and restored him with new sandals, a new robe, and a new ring on his finger. Forgiveness was instantaneous.

Dorothy Sayers has observed that "like the father of the prodigal son, God can see repentance coming a great way off and is there to meet it; the repentance is the reconciliation."

David now turns his attention to his listeners. "In light of my experience, here is what I call on you to do."

Verses 6, 7

"Therefore let everyone who is godly pray to you while you may be found; surely when the mighty waters rise, they will not reach him. You are my hiding place; you will protect me from trouble and surround me with songs of deliverance."

"Since your acceptance is guaranteed," David suggests, "why delay? Why not confess your sins now and receive the relief that forgiveness brings? Why not seek God today, while there is still life, and experience the peace that comes only from hiding in Him?" And then David asks that you pause and meditate on what he has just said—*Selah!*

This process is essential if we are ever to satisfy our hunger for God. As long as sin thrusts itself as a wall between God and us, we can never have intimacy with Him. Every brick of that wall must be torn down, every sin confessed, every remnant of self-sufficiency released. As Malcolm Muggeridge wrote: "Human beings are only bearable when the last defenses of their egos are down; when they stand, helpless and humbled, before the awful circumstances of their being. It is only thus that the point of the cross becomes clear, and the point of the cross is the point of life." We have no time for delay. Forgiveness and unabated access to the Father are available. Every moment we hesitate simply prolongs our agony. Now is the time!

It reminds me of the apostle Paul's admonition "I tell you, now is the time of God's favor, now is the day of salvation" (2 Cor. 6:2). The Holy Spirit does not know the word "tomorrow." His word is "today." Today is the day to come to Jesus. Today is the day to confess and receive forgiveness. And today is the day of salvation. But Satan's word is "delay."

I once heard Bruce Thielemann tell an old fable of how one day Satan grew concerned as he saw so many on earth coming to God, confessing their sins, and receiving salvation. So he called all the minions of hell together and said to them, "Who will go to earth and stem this tide? Who will go and what will you say to human beings in order that they will reject the salvation Jesus offers them?"

According to the legend, one foul creature approached to Satan and said, "I will go."

"What will you say to keep them from turning to God in repentance?"

"I will tell them there is no heaven," the fiend answered.

"You may not go, for there is a longing in every human heart for perfection," Satan objected. "Intuitively they know that there must be something better than their current condition. They will not believe you."

A second minion crawled from a dark place in hell and announced that he would go.

"And what will you tell the human race in order that it will reject the salvation offered by God?" Satan demanded.

"I will tell them that there is no hell," the creature explained.

"They will not believe you, either," Satan sneered. "For the Creator has placed in every human heart a sense of right and wrong. And with that sense there is a desire that the good will be rewarded and that the wicked will be punished. It is so deeply embedded in their consciousness that they will not believe you. You may not go."

Then a third demon, one worse even than the previous two, slithered out of the deepest, darkest part of hell and snarled, "I will go to earth."

"And what will you say?"

"I will tell them there is no hurry."

"Go," Satan told him.

That demon is still active in the earth today, telling us that there is still time. He encourages us to have our fun today, for there is plenty of time to repent at a later, more opportune moment. His counsel is deadly. But the Holy Spirit counters his message with a plea to respond to God today. Now is the moment of salvation. And to all those who heed that call, God fills them with encouragement.

Notice that the voice of the psalm has now changed from David's to God's. God says:

Verses 8–11
"I will instruct you and teach you in the way you should go; I will counsel you and watch over you. Do not be like the horse or the mule, which have no understanding but must be controlled by bit and bridle or they will not come to you. Many are the woes of the wicked, but the Lord's unfailing love surrounds the man who trusts in him. Rejoice in the Lord and be glad, you righteous; sing, all you who are upright in heart!"

This is the joy of all who respond to the call to repentance. God will instruct us in the way that we should live, and His unfailing love will surround us. Do you want to come closer to God? Begin by admitting your need of Him. Confess your sins to Him, and receive immediate and complete forgiveness for all of them today.

EXERCISES:

- ❖ Read Psalm 32 and pray that God will speak to your heart about your sins and that He will lead you to respond to His voice through repentance.
- ❖ Read 2 Corinthians 7:9, 10. Pray that God will give you "godly sorrow" for your sins. Pray that this will lead you to repentance.
- ❖ Pray Psalm 139. Pray that God, through the Holy Spirit, will reveal to you every sin that you need to confess. Once you have prayed, wait quietly until God brings particular sins to mind. Immediately after you recognize each sin, confess it and claim forgiveness.
- ❖ Make a commitment to end every day with a review of the previous 24 hours. As you think about your day, ask God to reveal to you the occasions you were obedient to His voice, as well as those you were not. Make a full confession of your failures for that day, and repent of each sin. Thank God for His forgiveness as you claim 1 John 1:9. Rejoice that God does not count your sins against you.
- ❖ James tells us to confess our faults to each other. In obedience to this command, prayerfully consider choosing a personal accountability partner. They should be someone of your gender, and someone who exhibits spiritual maturity. Confidentiality should also be a personal trait of the person. Agree to enter into a relationship of mutual accountability. Confess your areas of weakness and temptation to each other. Covenant together to pray for your partner about these areas of concern. Grant your accountability partner the right to ask you very pointed questions regarding these areas of your life, and determine to answer the questions honestly. When your partner shares an area of personal failure, follow the Spirit's lead in using confrontation, comfort, Scripture, and reassurances of forgiveness through God's grace. Use this relationship as a guard against sin.

CHAPTER 4

Thanksgiving

(Psalm 66)

In an address at the National Prayer Breakfast in 1994 Mother Teresa told of how one evening she, along with a number of other nuns, picked up four people from the street. Mother Theresa told the women, "You care for the other three. I will take responsibility for the one who looks the worst."

That patron of the poor, Mother Teresa, lovingly provided for the needs of the woman who was in the worst shape. After cleaning her up, she placed her in bed. The woman smiled beautifully, took Mother Teresa's hand, and said, "Thank you." Then she closed her eyes and died. Mother Teresa asked herself, "What would I say if I were in her place?" She concluded that she would have said that she was hungry, or in pain, or that she was dying, but she would not have said "Thank you." "But she gave me much more," Mother Teresa commented. "She gave me her grateful love. And she died with a smile on her face."

If you had been that dying woman, what would you have said? I'm not certain that I would have been able to thank anyone. I too would have focused on my needs, my pain, or my impending death. Gratitude would not have been high on my list of priorities. Do you have anything for which you should be thankful? You may feel that your life is at a low point, and as such, you have nothing for which to be thankful. But is that really true?

Perhaps you remember the story of Robinson Crusoe. When he was shipwrecked on a lonely island, he made two lists in opposing columns. On one side he stated that he had been cast onto a desolate island, but in the other column he noted that he was still alive and had not drowned, as

45

had happened to all others on board the ship. In the negative column he remarked that he was on a desolate island without human company, while in the positive column he admitted that he was not starving. It was a negative that he had no clothes, but it was very positive that he was in a tropical climate and did not need clothes. While he had no weapons of defense, he saw no wild beasts as he had observed on the coast of Africa, so he didn't really need a weapon. He had no one to carry on conversation with, but the wrecked ship had drifted so close to his island that he could salvage all his basic needs from it. Finally, Crusoe decided that as negative as many things were, he could still find a positive for which to be thankful.

Is such an attitude of gratitude a possibility in real life, or is it just the stuff of storybooks? Corrie ten Boom, in her autobiography, *The Hiding Place,* tells of the time she and her sister, Betsie, were forced to take off all their clothes during Nazi inspections at a death camp. A flood of emotions rushed over Corrie. She felt defiled, forsaken, and ashamed. Then something came to her mind, and with the thought came relief. *Jesus had been stripped of His clothes as He hung on the cross,* she reminded herself. In that moment she felt encouraged as she identified with the Savior. "Betsie, they took His clothes, too," she whispered to her sister.

Betsie gasped. "Oh, Corrie, and I never thanked Him."

For Helen Keller, thankfulness in the midst of adversity was no fairy tale. Despite having become deaf, mute, and blind at the age of 19 months, she could still write, "For three things I thank God every day of my life: thanks that He has vouchsafed me knowledge of His works; deep thanks that He has set in my darkness the lamp of faith; deep, deepest thanks that I have another life to look forward to—a life joyous with light and flowers and heavenly song."

Do you have anything to be thankful about? The psalmists learned to give thanks in all circumstances, whether positive or negative. Psalm 66 is a psalm of thanksgiving. In our quest to satisfy our hunger for God, thanksgiving is an important step to that intimacy we so earnestly desire. And Psalm 66 helps us understand how giving thanks brings us closer to God.

Psalm 66:1-4

"Shout with joy to God, all the earth! Sing the glory of his name; make his praise glorious! Say to God, 'How awesome are your deeds! So great is your power that your enemies cringe before you. All the earth bows down to you; they sing praise to you, they sing praise to your name.'"

THANKSGIVING

The psalmist calls for the entire earth to shout praises to God. He tells us that we are to give thanks to God for His mighty deeds. He leaves no one out. Everyone is to sing praise to God—everyone is to give Him thanks. The first reason for thanksgiving is that of God's awesome power—power so great that His enemies cringe before Him. But that is not all. The psalm tells us that we are to sing and shout thanks to God for His work in nature.

Verses 5-7
"Come and see what God has done, how awesome his works in man's behalf! He turned the sea into dry land, they passed through the waters on foot—come, let us rejoice in him. He rules forever by his power, his eyes watch the nations—let not the rebellious rise up against him."

The power of nature mystifies us. Scientists attempt to control nature, but their efforts are futile. In recent months we have seen earthquakes, brush and forest fires, tornadoes, hurricanes, tsunamis, and the devastation such natural disasters bring. We stand in awe of their power, helpless to do much but flee from their path.

I live in Texas, and many people tell me they would not move there because of their fear of tornadoes. Many of my Texas friends reject the idea of living in California because of its earthquakes, mudslides, and brush fires. My California friends avoid Florida because of its hurricanes. And I have friends in Florida who will not move to Minnesota because of its freezing temperatures and blizzards.

We are all in awe of the power of nature, and at times we fear it. But when we think of the God who not only created nature but also has the power to control it, our minds boggle and our knees knock. We are left with nothing but praise for such a mighty deity.

When, on December 26, 2004, a 9.1 magnitude earthquake and resulting tsunami hit the Indian Ocean, causing more than 150,000 deaths, people began to wonder what God might be saying through this disaster. Was it a divine judgment or a warning of ominous things to come? Opinions differ. Whatever the case, the psalmist tells us to praise God for His power over nature. The psalm's opening verses tell us that we are to shout, sing, praise, offer thanks, and rejoice. We are to do all of this to "the glory of his name." In particular the psalmist tells us to sing as an act of praise and worship to God.

Nothing evokes such strong emotions as does music. Music reaches to our souls and elicits sadness, elation, and everything in between. Christians have always been a people who love to sing. We cannot help singing praises to God! And we sing of His redemption and of His soon return, when we will be with Him forever.

When music pours forth from God's people in response to His working in their lives, the emotions can be overwhelming. But music in worship should not be just about the expression of our emotions, or that music would be focused on us. Rather music in worship should always be about God. It is a natural and proper reaction to His goodness, His power, and His salvation. Music is to give glory to Him. Isn't that what the psalmist is saying in the opening verses of this psalm?

Verses 1–3

"Shout with joy to God, all the earth! Sing the glory of his name; make his praise glorious! Say to God, 'How awesome are your deeds! So great is your power that your enemies cringe before you.'"

These first three verses mix two different forms of worship. One consists of praise and the other of thanksgiving. Praise generally focuses on God's characteristics. In verse 3 we praise Him for His power. He possesses power, or omnipotence, whether He uses it or not. So we exalt Him as a deity of power. We also extol Him for His grace, His knowledge (omniscience), His justice, and so on. However, when God uses one of His characteristics to perform an act on our behalf, then we give thanks. Verse 5 clues us in to this.

Verse 5

"Come and see what God has done, how awesome his works in man's behalf!"

Then the psalmist goes on to describe how God delivered His people from Pharaoh's army by allowing them to pass through the Red Sea. For this the biblical writer is grateful. God has delivered you and He has delivered me. I can point to specific instances and say, "God intervened here in my behalf." He has also delivered me at other times of which I am unaware. The Lord has done things for me that I don't know about. Thanksgiving is showing gratitude to God for all these, whether seen or unseen.

In the case of divine rescue from Pharaoh's army, the event was observable and miraculous, and involved intervention against the usual laws of nature. God parted the waters of the Red Sea and allowed His people to pass through unharmed. So the psalmist thanks Him for deliverance and for the fact that He used His power over nature to save His people.

The first seven verses of this psalm tell us that everyone on the face of the earth is called to worship God through the giving of praise and thanksgiving. Among the reasons for our praise and thanksgiving are those of His power over nature and His salvation of His people. Now look at verses 8–12.

Verses 8-12

"Praise our God, O peoples, let the sound of his praise be heard; he has preserved our lives and kept our feet from slipping. For you, O God, tested us; you refined us like silver. You brought us into prison and laid burdens on our backs. You let men ride over our heads; we went through fire and water, but you brought us to a place of abundance."

The first seven verses are a universal summons to worship God. Now the call narrows and more specifically aims at God's covenant people—those who have chosen to enter into relationship with Him. The command to all the land to sing praise to God is an invitation to look from the outside in—to view God's deliverance of His people and honor Him for it.

Now the psalmist addresses the people who viewed this episode from the inside. Their forebears actually experienced that salvation. They are to sing of their deliverance in a more personal manner.

Those not in covenant relationship with God can look on from the outside and be amazed by what they see. But those who live in covenant relationship have experienced His love and salvation firsthand. Therefore, the psalmist now uses first personal plural pronouns to describe his praise for God:

Verses 8, 9

"Praise our God . . . ; he has preserved our lives and kept our feet from slipping."

It is a deeply personal experience for the psalmist and for all who claim to live in relationship with God. As I read verse 12, however, some questions arise.

Verse 12

"You let men ride over our heads; we went through fire and water, but you brought us to a place of abundance."

At times the Lord allows us to receive the consequences of our choices, and that means that trouble may come upon us. It is not that He wants us to experience difficulty, but He often permits it as the direct result of our choices, those of our leaders, or those around us. But even then God does not forsake us.

When the psalmist says, "We went through fire and water, but you brought us to a place of abundance," he means, "Come hell or high water, You have seen us through." The trouble we may be enduring today may leave us wondering if God could possibly love us. But the psalmist reassures us of God's love and tells us that He will see us through our present difficulties. Give thanks to Him for His mighty power in our lives. For some it is difficult. They find it a near impossibility to say a simple "Thanks."

A farmer was sitting on the porch with his wife one evening in Vermont. As he sat there he looked at her and began to realize just how much that wonderful, faithful woman meant to him. They had been married for 42 years, and she had been such a marvelous help as they raised a family and worked their farm together. Overcome with emotion, the farmer said, "Wife, you've been such a wonderful woman that there are times that it's all I can do to keep from telling you." Many of us are a whole lot like that old farmer. God has been so good to us, but we manage to refrain from telling Him (or anyone else, for that matter)!

Psalm 66 summons us to tell God that we appreciate all that He has done for us. As His people we can find reasons to thank Him even when others may think that calamity has overtaken us.

Matthew Henry was a famous English Bible scholar. On one occasion thieves attacked and robbed him of his money. In his diary he commented on the incident: "Let me be thankful. First, I was never robbed before. Second, although they took my purse, they didn't take my life. Third, although they took my all, it was not much. Fourth, let me be thankful because it was I who was robbed and not I who did the robbing."

In all things, positive and negative, God's people will find reasons to offer thanks.

Erwin W. Lutzer writes: "It's only when we choose to give praise for the rough spots in life that we begin to see them from God's perspective. If we don't give thanks in all things, we are living in unbelief, for we are assuming that our circumstances are not controlled by a God who loves us! I'm not saying that you should give thanks for sin, but you can thank God for how He will use that sin to teach, to rebuke, or to challenge you."

The psalmist urges all of us to thank God in all things. Doing so is a marvelous tool for drawing closer to God and satisfying our hunger for Him. Even when His people have made poor choices and brought calamity on themselves, they are to thank Him, because He will use it for their good and for His glory. God intervenes, rescues His people, and brings something good from the experience. At other times it may not be God's people who make poor decisions, but others in authority over their lives who cause disaster for them. Even then He can bring good from the evil that befalls His people.

Take, for instance, a case that comes to us from Japan. August 9, 2005, marked the sixtieth anniversary of the bombing of Nagasaki. In 1945 Nagasaki was the center of Japanese Christianity. A significant community of Christians lived there and had survived more than 300 years of persecution. Many had been martyred for their faith. Worship services had to meet in secrecy. Only about 40 years prior to the dropping of the bomb on Nagasaki had they been allowed to worship openly. Then, on August 9, 1945, an atomic bomb wiped out that community of Christians. The surviving Christians had an unexpected response to the tragedy.

Takashi Nagai lost his wife from radiation sickness during the weeks after the dropping of the bomb on his city. He said that the 8,000 Christians who died instantly in the blast had perished for the cause of freedom in the world. "Let us give thanks that through this sacrifice peace was given to the world and freedom of religion to Japan," he said.

I stand in awe of such faith. Even in the midst of such a horrific tragedy, these Christians found reason to offer thanks to God. The Lord uses the circumstances of our lives—both positive and negative—in order to make His will known to the world. Those who love Him and live in relationship with Him will find in all circumstances of life reason to give thanks and to sing praises to His name.

The first half of Psalm 66 urges the entire world to sing praise to God, and then it calls for His people to shout thanksgiving. But in verse 13 the focus narrows further, and the psalm becomes much more personal.

Verses 13–15

"I will come to your temple with burnt offerings and fulfill my vows to you—vows my lips promised and my mouth spoke when I was in trouble. I will sacrifice fat animals to you and an offering of rams; I will offer bulls and goats."

The pronouns have now become first person singular. "I will come to your temple . . . [to] fulfill my vows to you." It is one thing to call the en-

51

tire world to praise God, and another yet to summon His covenant people to praise Him. But the most important call is the one that God makes to each one of us individually to give Him thanks.

Verse 13 mentions burnt offerings. In what were referred to as "fellowship" offerings the fire of the altar consumed only a portion of them while the worshipper and his friends shared the remainder. Eating such an offering became, so to speak, an occasion for a religious celebration.

The fire of the altar, however, entirely consumed the burnt offerings. A burnt offering was more serious, indicating a more complete dedication of the worshipper to God. This is what the psalmist implies here. He is making a full surrender of himself before the Lord because of His deliverance in the time of trouble.

Verse 15 tells us that the offering will consist of rams, bulls, and goats—more than one of each type of animal. A very costly offering, it indicates that the psalmist realized that his response to God must be in proportion to the deliverance he has received. A great deliverance requires a great response. The most powerful acknowledgment of our thankfulness that we can make today is the offering of our very lives.

Verses 16–20

"Come and listen, all you who fear God; let me tell you what he has done for me. I cried out to him with my mouth; his praise was on my tongue. If I had cherished sin in my heart, the Lord would not have listened; but God has surely listened and heard my voice in prayer. Praise be to God, who has not rejected my prayer or withheld his love from me!"

Here is the psalmist's personal testimony. When he experienced the hand of God in his life—when the Lord saved him from a great calamity—he did not keep quiet. Wanting everyone to know how wonderful His God was, He told everyone who would listen of God's marvelous deliverance in his life. It is still another way of giving thanks to God. But thanksgiving does not come easily for us. We do not seem to be hardwired to naturally offer it. More often, our natural tendency is to complain.

In some parts of Mexico hot and cold springs occur side by side, and because of the convenience of the natural phenomenon the women often bring their laundry and boil their clothes in the hot springs and then rinse them in the cold ones. A man watching them at work commented to his Mexican friend and guide, "I imagine that they think old Mother Nature is pretty generous to supply such ample, clean hot and cold water here side by side for their free use."

"Not really," the guide answered. "Instead, they tend to grumble quite a bit that Mother Nature does not supply soap." Human beings are quite ingenious. We can always find something to gripe about.

A man was standing at a desk in the post office addressing an envelope when an older individual approached him. The older man held a postcard in his hand and asked, "Sir, could you please address this postcard for me?" The first man was happy to do so, and also wrote a short message for the gentleman. He even signed it for him. Then he asked the older man, "Now, is there anything else I can do for you?"

The old fellow thought about it for a minute, then said, "Yes. At the end could you just put 'PS: Please excuse the sloppy handwriting'?"

How much better it is if we choose a positive attitude—an attitude of thanksgiving and praise!

John Henry Jowett, a British preacher of an earlier generation, once wrote: "Gratitude is a vaccine, an antitoxin, and an antiseptic." He meant that gratitude functions like a vaccine in that it can prevent the invasion of a disgruntled, discouraged spirit. Gratitude acts like an antitoxin in that it can prevent the effects of the poisons of cynicism, criticalness, and grumbling. And like an antiseptic, gratitude can soothe and heal the most troubled spirit. Thankfulness leaves no room for discouragement.

I once read a legend of a man who found the barn where Satan kept his seeds ready to be sown in the human heart. He began to look through all the different types of seeds until he found the seeds of discouragement. They were more numerous than all others. One of Satan's imps told the man that those seeds would grow almost anywhere. However, there was one place where Satan had never been able to get seeds of discouragement to thrive: the heart of a grateful person. The habits of thanksgiving and praise will change lives.

An article by Willis P. King in *Christianity Today* stated that "gratitude" derives from the same root word as "grace," which signifies the free and boundless mercy of God. Also, "thanks" has the same root word as "think," so that to think is to thank. How amazing is it that just thinking about the abundant grace of God in our lives can have such a powerful effect in us!

Martin Luther King, Sr., said that his mother had told him to always thank God for whatever was left. Now, that is something to consider. Even if all that you have is just enough breath to complain, you still have something left.

Some years later the senior Dr. King had lost his wife, who had been shot to death right before his eyes at the organ in Atlanta's Ebenezer church, the church where he served as pastor. In addition, he eventually lost his two sons, A. D. King and Martin Luther King, Jr. After all that pain and all those losses, he could still say, "Thank God for what's left. There's always enough left in life to make it worth living."

I'm convinced that most of the spiritual poverty we experience results from our failure to give thanks to God. The prayer of thanksgiving is more important than the prayer of request—it is more important to say to God "thanks" than it is to say "please."

If you are hungry for God—if your soul is famished for want of Him—may I suggest that you develop the habit of giving thanks? You will find that this simple act will draw you closer to the One who will satisfy your soul's hunger.

A simple woman from the Appalachian Mountains chiseled this epitaph on her husband's tombstone: "He always appreciated."

Oh, but that this could be the epitaph for every Christian! How different would our lives be! Our hunger for God would be satisfied if we would continuously cry with the psalmist: "Praise be to God, who has not rejected my prayer or withheld His love from me!"

EXERCISES:

❖ Commit yourself to thank God daily for His many blessings. Make a list of your blessings and read them often and give thanks.

❖ Read Psalm 66. What are the things that all humanity should praise God for? What things should His people especially praise Him for? And what are the things that you personally should praise Him for? Thank God for those things often.

❖ Use Psalms 146-150 as your morning prayers, praying one of the psalms each day for five days. On the sixth and seventh days, using the patterns you learned in Psalms 146-150, write your own psalms of prayer.

❖ Determine to make praise and thanksgiving integral parts of every prayer, devoting at least two thirds of the time to giving thanks and praising God.

CHAPTER 5

Worship

(Psalm 95)

Sir Hall Caine wrote the novel *The Scapegoat*. In it he describes a little girl named Naomi who was deaf, mute, and blind. In the middle of the night she would awaken and walk into her father's room. She was not ill or in pain, and she had not experienced a nightmare. Once in the room she would touch him, but not to awaken him or get his attention. The child simply stood beside his bed lightly touching her father in order that she might know that he was near.

Naomi cherished the love and care of her father, and she longed for the reassurance that he was still there and that she belonged. So she just stood in his presence, gazing, with her fingers, upon the man who made her feel loved and accepted.

A. W. Tozer wrote: "More spiritual progress can be made in one short moment of speechless silence in the awesome presence of God than in years of mere study."

Have you ever stood in speechless silence in the presence of your heavenly Father—not because you were ill or had any other emergency, but simply to be reassured of His loving acceptance? We have been studying the Psalms in order to learn how to satisfy our hunger for God—to learn how we might draw closer to Him. One of the most important ways to accomplish this is through worship.

Former United States president Calvin Coolidge wrote that "it is only when men begin to worship that they begin to grow."

What is worship and how is it done?

Allow me once again to turn to A. W. Tozer. "There are delights that the heart may enjoy in the awesome presence of God that cannot find expression in language; they belong to the unutterable element in Christian experience. Not many enjoy them because not many know that they can. The whole concept of ineffable worship has been lost."

Among other things, worship is standing in the presence of the Almighty and finding assurance of His love and acceptance. It is learning that in spite of our foibles and failures, He declares that we really do belong to Him. One place in which we discover this is in Psalm 95, a psalm that instructs us in the art of worship.

Psalm 95:1, 2

"Come, let us sing for joy to the Lord; let us shout aloud to the Rock of our salvation. Let us come before him with thanksgiving and extol him with music and song."

Worship is indispensable for anyone who would satisfy his hunger for God. Gerald Vann observed that "worship is not a part of the Christian life; it is the Christian life." If this is true, it is no wonder that so many professed Christians still have a deep, unsatisfied hunger for God. For the most part, worship is a lost art. Psalm 95 provides instruction for those who would rediscover the art of worship. The author begins by describing joyous worship. He calls us to "sing for joy," to "shout aloud," and to approach God "with thanksgiving and extol him with music and song."

The passage does not seek to be an exclusive description of worship, but illustrates one important style. Worship can take place in silence and darkness. It is not always necessary to display emotion in our worship, but it is natural and appropriate to worship God with great emotion and expression. The psalmist reveals to us several forms of worship that those who would know God can enjoy as they seek Him. First, he tells us that we are to sing.

Both the Old and New Testaments include singing as a vital element of worship. It is said that only the Christian faith has hymnals. We have them because we truly have something to sing about! We sing to express the joy of our salvation! True biblical religion is joyous religion, and nothing can express joy better than singing. We sing the praise of the One who has so graciously provided salvation for us.

A second form of worship presented here is to shout. Earlier, I quoted A. W. Tozer, who spoke of the value of silence in God's presence. While silence is an appropriate form of worship, so too is shouting. Some people are uncomfortable with the latter, and it is just fine if we do not shout. I grew up in two different congregations that we could best describe as "shout-free zones." Not only did we not shout; we tended to look down on those who did!

Scripture, however, tells me that shouting can be a perfectly appropriate form of worship. Therefore, I have no business feeling superior to those who choose to do so. In fact, since I have come to an understanding of this scriptural principal, I've been known to do a little shouting myself!

Next, according to Psalm 95 we are to worship with music. We have already said that singing is to be a part of worship, but the psalmist here has in mind musical instruments. Which instruments? While Psalm 95 does not mention any specific ones, Psalm 150 refers to trumpets, harps, lyres, tambourines, strings, flutes, and cymbals. I cannot think of any musical instruments mentioned in Scripture that have been left out of Psalm 150's list. Such would seem to imply that we can use any instrument to worship God. Scripture does not give us a list of "holy" instruments and another of "unholy" ones. The Bible mentions percussion instruments as well as more melodic examples. It is permissible to use any musical instrument in the worship of our God.

Finally, the psalmist says that words are a form of worship. Not just our words, but God's words as well. We come to church to read and hear Scripture. This is important since it is the most reliable source of information we have regarding the object of our worship—God. Scripture also tells us why we are to worship. In the Bible we learn of our appropriate reaction to God's words in Scripture—we are to respond through obedience to them. In addition to God's words, we are to use our own words to express adoration and praise, making a verbal response to His words to us. Thus worship involves singing, shouting, instrumental music, human words, and God's words.

I mentioned that Scripture tells us why we are to worship God. One place we find the reason for worship is in verses 3 through 5 of Psalm 95.

Verses 3-5

"For the Lord is the great God, the great King above all gods. In his hand are the depths of the earth, and the mountain peaks belong to him. The sea is his, for he made it, and his hands formed the dry land."

We are to worship God because of His greatness. But to do that, we must first understand something of what He is like—sense something of His power, majesty, holiness, justice, mercy, and love. The starting point for our worship is a realization of the fact that He is the Creator.

Repeatedly, from Genesis to Revelation, the Bible calls us to worship God as the Creator, and to bow in awe before Him because of His creative power. In fact, God justifies His demand that we worship Him by reminding us that He created us.

The fourth commandment—the Sabbath commandment—involves the celebration of a weekly anniversary of Creation. Thus Genesis tied worship, and even the day of worship, to Creation. That same theme continues throughout Scripture until in Revelation 14, in what many have described as God's last great message to our world, the Creation theme reemerges. It tells us to "fear God and give him glory, because the hour of his judgment has come. Worship him who made the heavens, the earth, the sea and the springs of water" (Rev. 14:7). From Genesis to Revelation Scripture grounds the call for worship in the fact that God is Creator.

A second reason for worship appears in verses 6 and 7 of Psalm 95.

Verses 6, 7

"Come, let us bow down in worship, let us kneel before the Lord our Maker; for he is our God and we are the people of his pasture, the flock under his care."

We are also to worship because God is our shepherd. Scripture here cites His relationship to His people as a reason to worship Him. While the creative power of God is important, it is also a bit impersonal. However, when we think of Him as our shepherd, worship comes closer to home. Because He is our shepherd, we are "the flock under his care."

As we learned in chapter 2, the shepherd and his flock had an intense relationship. Sheep depended upon the shepherd for everything: protection, food, water, healing, and rest. They are defenseless and helpless creatures. The shepherd is present at all times to protect the sheep and care for their basic needs of food and water. It was the shepherd who tended to wounds and kept the animals free of parasites. He recognized that his sheep were fearful of certain things, and worked to minimize those terrors. Thus the relationship between shepherd and sheep was one of tender concern and care. It is how God cares for you.

Jesus says that He is the Good Shepherd. We are the flock under His care. A good shepherd lays down his or her life for the sheep. Jesus did just that for us. The psalmist cites such a personal relationship as another reason for our worship.

We need to note one more thing in verses 6 and 7. The psalmist introduces the idea of reverence before God. He tells us to "bow down" as we

58

worship God. The Hebrew means literally "to prostrate oneself." Humbling ourselves before Him, we admit our need of Him and glorify Him as the only one who is worthy of our worship. Writing a century ago, Alexander Patterson Smith observed that "to worship God is to make Him the supreme object of our esteem and delight, both in public, private, and secret."

Albert Thorwaldsen, a sculptor, created a famous statue of Christ. Having finished his work, he invited a friend to see it. The statue portrayed Jesus Christ with His arms outstretched and His head bowed. After looking at the figure, the friend commented, "I can't see His face."

"If you want to see the face of Christ," Thorwaldsen replied, "you must get on your knees." Only when we worship as servants on bended knee can we clearly see the face of Jesus.

A French proverb states, "A good meal ought to begin with hunger." If you are not hungry, it does not matter that the food is fit for a king. But when you are famished, almost anything tastes good. God has designed that each of us should hunger for Him. Worship is one of the ways we respond to our hunger for God.

George Eliot wrote that "the first condition of human goodness is something to love; the second, something to reverence." We are to worship God with singing, shouting, instrumental music, human words, and God's words. Furthermore, we are to worship Him because He is our Creator and because He lives in intimate relationship with us, much as a shepherd does with the sheep. And when we worship God, we are to come in all reverence and humility. To know God is to reverence Him.

President Theodore Roosevelt was an ardent naturalist who loved the great outdoors. While camping with the naturalist William Beebe, he and Beebe would step outside their tent and gaze into a sky filled with brilliant stars. When they would find the lower left-hand corner of Pegasus—a faint speck of light—Roosevelt would then recite, "That is the spiral galaxy in Andromeda. It is as large as our Milky Way. It is one of 100 million galaxies. It consists of 100 billion suns, each larger than our sun." Next they would pause in the silence, allowing all that they had seen and said to sink in. Finally Roosevelt would announce, "Now I think we feel small enough! Let's go to bed."

When we come to worship God, we must do so in all humility. He is God, and we are not. He is the Creator, and we are His creatures. We are to humble ourselves as we worship Him.

Recently I saw Joni Eareckson Tada at a convention for religious broadcasters. Mrs. Tada became a quadriplegic through a diving accident at age 17. One time she attended a convention at which the speaker closed his message with an appeal for everyone to kneel in prayer. The only one not able to kneel, she began to weep openly. She longed to physically kneel before her Lord. At that moment she prayed, "Lord Jesus, I can't wait for the day when I will rise up on resurrected legs. The first thing I will then do is to drop on grateful, glorified knees and worship You."

True worshippers humble themselves before God. They acknowledge that He is sovereign and that we are His people. He alone is worthy of our worship.

What is worship? Perhaps it is easier to begin with what it is not. Worship is not just introspection; otherwise, we would worship our feelings. It is not some ecstatic glow, or we would worship that. Nor is it just listening to a sermon or singing a hymn, as helpful as these things might be. Recognizing our sin, we see, in worship, our need and are brought to a point of humility. True worship acknowledges our inability to do anything in our own strength. Thus it is an activity that points away from us to Someone greater. Concentrating our attention on Him, it praises Him—adores Him. In addition, it focuses on Scripture, since the Bible is God-breathed. And then worship responds with obedience.

In Psalm 95 we find a warning for the worshipper. Look especially at the last part of verse 7.

Verses 7–11

"Today, if you hear his voice, do not harden your hearts as you did at Meribah, as you did that day at Massah in the desert, where your fathers tested and tried me, though they had seen what I did. For forty years I was angry with that generation; I said, 'They are a people whose hearts go astray, and they have not known my ways.' So I declared on oath in my anger, 'They shall never enter my rest.'"

The incident mentioned here involves something that happened when Israel wandered in the desert. They came to a place called Rephidim, but it lacked water, a serious matter.

Moses had charge of a large company of people with extensive flocks. The desert is a hot, dry place, and to be without water means certain death. The people became highly contentious over the issue. Even though they had seen the deliverance that God had provided from Egypt, and even though they had seen Him part the Red Sea, they failed to trust Him in this new matter. So God told Moses to strike a rock at Horeb, and from that He would bring water. When Moses did as commanded, the water flowed. It was a place named Massah, which means "testing." It also had a second name, Meribah, or "quarreling." Forever after the place would symbolize a failure to trust God—a failure to obey Him. Years later a similar incident occurred at Kadesh, and even though God provided water there, it also received the name Meribah.

The psalmist points to these incidents to illustrate that Israel's disobedience prevented them from entering the Promised Land. That same attitude is abroad today in the hearts of many. But true worship transforms that spirit. The biblical writer warns us that true worship always results in a difference in the worshipper. It produces obedience. Richard Foster comments that "if worship does not change us, it has not been worship. To stand before the Holy One of eternity is to change. Worship begins in holy expectancy; it ends in holy obedience."

The author of Hebrews quotes this psalm. While the psalm deals with the entrance of Israel into the Promised Land, the author of Hebrews uses it to illustrate entering into God's rest. God had promised rest to His people. We receive His rest, in part today, as we trust in Him for our salvation. Ultimately we fully gain it when we enter heaven. We are told that "there remains, then, a Sabbath-rest for the people of God; for anyone who enters God's rest also rests from his own work, just as God did from his" (Heb. 4:9, 10).

A European explorer in Africa, eager to press ahead on his journey, paid his porters extra for a series of forced marches. When they were almost within reach of their destination, the porters stopped and refused to go forward. The explorer offered more money, but no amount could persuade them. When asked why, they said they had to wait for their souls to catch up.

Worship enables us to rest from work as we allow our souls to catch up. We rest from the task of earning our own salvation. Jesus has already won it for us. As a result, we should rest in the knowledge that our salvation is secure, a fact that should cause our worship to change us. Because we have been redeemed, and because we worship our holy God, we should then be different people. Worship implies a full surrender to the lordship of Jesus in our lives. When we submit to His lordship, we'll give Him our worship.

Finally, notice that Psalm 95:7 tells us that we are to listen to God's voice today. "Today, if you hear his voice . . ." Today is the day of salvation. Now is the time to believe and follow Jesus.

I believe that worship begins in silence as we listen to God's voice through Scripture. Our temptation is to speak, shout, sing, or make music too quickly. We tend to make noise when what we really need is to be still and recognize that He is God.

When we do respond, it must be based on the Word of God. We must hear His Word, and then we must obey it. Until we do that, we have nothing for which to praise Him. Praise has value only when educated by the Word of God. Therefore, worship is the process of hearing the Word of God, obeying it, and then praising God for it. Or as David Julius said: "Worship is pictured at its best in Isaiah when the young prophet became aware of the Father; aware of his own limitations; aware of the Father's directives; and aware of the task at hand."

You may have noticed that I frequently quote A. W. Tozer, a pastor and author whose work I love. Tozer died in the early 1960s, but his work stands the test of time and is, I believe, as insightful today as it was the day he wrote it. Read what he has to say about worship: "We are called to an everlasting preoccupation with God."

During the fifth and sixth centuries an order of monks in Eastern Europe called "the sleepless ones" sang and prayed in relays, thus assuring a continuous, nonstop service of praise to God. In their own small way they were giving a foretaste of what happens in heaven—a holy preoccupation with God. John the revelator pictures 24 elders and four heavenly creatures singing night and day without stopping, "Holy, holy, holy is the Lord God Almighty" (Rev. 4:8). The 24 elders and the four heavenly creatures have "an everlasting preoccupation with God." Someday we will join their song, but until we do, we need to learn to worship in the here and now.

Worship is the next best thing to being in God's physical presence. Spiritually, that is exactly what we do—we come into His presence when we worship. And as we do we receive a promise—the promise that one day our hunger for God will be satisfied. The Lord will satisfy our God hunger as we continually sing His praises in His presence forever. Because, just being there—standing there and gazing upon Him, even if we do so in silence—will be enough to reassure us that we really do belong, that we really are accepted, and that we really are His children forever.

We get small tastes of that heavenly experience whenever we worship Him in spirit and truth. First, we see Him high and exalted, the King of kings and Lord of lords. We recognize that He is our Creator and we are His creatures. Then we confront the fact that He is altogether holy, and we are sinners. That demonstrates to us that we stand in danger of being consumed by our sin. But as we realize that Jesus has redeemed us, our tongues will spontaneously burst into praise to Him! "Holy, holy, holy, Lord God Almighty."

Peter Buehler helped lead John and Charles Wesley to experience conversion. Once, while in conversation with Charles, Peter said, "If I had a thousand tongues, I'd praise Christ with them all." Charles Wesley took that stray comment and created the hymn "O for a Thousand Tongues to Sing." I end this chapter with the words to that hymn.

> "O for a thousand tongues to sing
> My great Redeemer's praise,
> The glories of my God and King,
> The triumphs of His grace!
>
> "My gracious Master and my God,
> Assist me to proclaim,
> To spread through all the earth abroad
> The honors of Thy name.
>
> "Jesus! the name that charms our fears,
> That bids our sorrows cease;
> 'Tis music in the sinners' ears,
> 'Tis life, and health, and peace.
>
> "He breaks the power of canceled sin,
> He sets the prisoner free;
> His blood can make the foulest clean;
> His blood availed for me."

EXERCISES:

Richard Foster, in his book, *Celebration of Discipline,* lists several steps to effective worship. They are:

1. "Learn to practice the presence of God daily." This consists of living in Christ every moment of every day as we learn to listen to His whisperings. It also involves times of inner worship, confession, Bible study, and contemplation.
2. "Have many different experiences of worship." Have private wor-

ship every day. To this we should add worship in small groups of two or three using Bible study, prayer, and praise. Complete your week by attending corporate worship at church. You will find that the private and small group worship experiences will prepare you for a richer worship at church.

3. "Find ways to really help prepare for the gathered experience." Foster suggests such things as going to bed early the night before church, having a time of inward examination and confession, going over hymns and scriptures that will be used in church, and arriving at church beforehand for a time of quiet meditation.

4. "Have a willingness to be gathered in the power of the Lord." Here we change our focus from our personal agendas to the corporate good. Submitting to the ways of God and to those with whom we enjoy Christian fellowship, we pray for God to pour His Spirit upon the assembled body.

5. "Cultivate holy dependency." Trust in God's power, rather than your own, to make something of value happen in worship. Watch for His moving.

6. "Absorb distractions with gratitude." Greet noise and other distractions with blessing and praise rather than resentment. Bless children who make noise. Receive whatever happens with openness and joy.

7. "Learn to offer a sacrifice of worship." Even when you don't feel like worshipping, worship anyway. Declare that the people with whom you worship are your people. Give your worship as a pleasing sacrifice before the Lord.

Foster further lists avenues into worship. He suggests that we: cease all humanly initiated activity as we allow God to lead; engage in heartfelt praise; incorporate singing as a vital part of worship; and involve body, mind, spirit, and emotions in the act of worship.

❖ Read Psalm 95 again. List your reasons for worshipping God.

❖ Make specific plans for improving your worship experiences. Include private, small group, and corporate activities as a part of your plan.

CHAPTER 6

Community

(Psalm 133)

I enjoyed the PBS's television broadcast of *The Three Tenors* a number of years ago. Jose Carreras, Placido Domingo, and Luciano Pavarotti united their immense talents to create a memorable performance for that broadcast. These three world-class operatic tenors are each immensely proud of their own accomplishments. While I do not know any of them, it is my observation that most people at the top of their field, as are these three men, quite often carry immense egos and are extremely competitive. When a reporter from The *Atlantic Monthly* tried to press the issue of competitiveness between the three men, Placido Domingo replied, "You have to put all your concentration into opening your heart to the music. You can't be rivals when you're together making music."

What is true of music is even more so of Christians. If we Christians are going to be what God wants us to be, we must open our hearts to the music of heaven. We will need to learn to work together in harmony to make His music in this world. So often Christians have failed in this. We appear to be rivals rather than partners. Everyone wants to sing a solo, and no one wants to sing harmony.

"Interestingly, of all the songs in the book of Revelation," Graham Kendrick noted, "not one is a solo. The 24 elders sing and cast their crowns before His feet, the united voices of countless angels resound, every living creature in heaven and earth and under the earth and all that is in them are joined in one song. Those who are victorious over the beast are given harps and a song to sing. In every case multitudes of people or angels unite in the same song with absolute unity."

When the church is more of a collection of soloists than a great choir, we fail to fulfill Jesus' vision for His followers. That involves becoming a loving community of believers. Jesus said: "A new command I give you: Love one another. As I have loved you, so you must love one another. By this all men will know that you are my disciples, if you love one another" (John 13:34, 35). Our Savior intended that love, mutual support, and genuine community would be the identifying characteristics of His church. Until it observes such things in the church, the world will not take us seriously.

Francis Schaeffer explained that "we cannot expect the world to believe that the Father sent the Son, that Jesus' claims are true, and that Christianity is true, unless the world sees some reality of the oneness of true Christians. Now that is frightening. Should we not feel some emotion at this point?"

The psalms have something to say on this subject. One of the most beautiful poems in Scripture is Psalm 133—a poem of community.

Psalm 133

"A song of ascents. Of David. How good and pleasant it is when brothers live together in unity! It is like precious oil poured on the head, running down on the beard, running down on Aaron's beard, down upon the collar of his robes. It is as if the dew of Hermon were falling on Mount Zion. For there the Lord bestows his blessing, even life forevermore."

Notice that the psalm has the heading "A song of ascents." The phrase begins Psalms 120 through 134. Eugene H. Peterson tells us that Israelites prayed and sang these 15 psalms as they traveled to Jerusalem to worship. Throughout the year several special worship services convened in Jerusalem at the Temple. People came to the city from throughout Palestine, as well as the surrounding countries, to worship during such services. Usually they would travel in groups in order to provide greater safety from thieves, wild animals, and other hazards.

Jerusalem perches on top of a hill in a range of hills, so the people would ascend to Jerusalem for such religious celebrations. As they climbed toward Jerusalem they would sing or recite psalms as a preparation to their worship. Thus people referred to the psalms most commonly sung at this time as "the psalms of ascents." Located near the end of this sequence of 15 psalms, Psalm 133 depicts the desired condition of God's people as they start their worship. Our purpose in this book is to learn how to draw close to God. One of the tools we use for this purpose is that of Christian community. Patrick Morley commented that "the height of our love for God will never exceed the depth of our love for one another." So Christian community is necessary if we are to satisfy our hunger for God. Psalm 133 begins by presenting the goal of community.

Verse 1
"How good and pleasant it is when brothers live together in unity!"

The goal is to live in unity with our fellow believers. Community is essential for Christians. I cannot find anything in Scripture that calls us to solo Christianity. Christians are always summoned to be members of a community. God never works with individuals in isolation, but always with people in relationship.

When God created Adam and Eve, He instructed each not to leave the other's side. They were to remain in community, for there they would find their strength. God gathered together a special people, a holy nation, to fulfill His purposes. Jesus worked with 12 disciples, and even when He sent them out to work, He dispatched them in twos. Acts 2:1 and 5:12 tell us that the church first formed when 120 people had gathered together in one place. The book of Hebrews addressed the problems of church members by admonishing them: "not neglecting to meet together, as is the habit of some, but encouraging one another, and all the more as you see the Day drawing near" (Heb. 10:25, ESV). Even the Godhead—the Father, Son, and Holy Spirit—work in community. Community is essential for the Christian. It strengthens and protects us and implies a social dimension to even the religious life.

Crowds of people sang Psalm 133 as they journeyed to Jerusalem for worship. As Eugene H. Peterson reminds us: "Everyone shared a common purpose, traveling a common path, striving toward a common goal, that path and purpose and goal being God. How much better than making the long trip alone!"

But it is not easy to live in community. Anyone who grew up with siblings realizes that brothers and sisters fight. The first story in the Bible about brothers is that of Cain and Abel and how Cain murdered his brother out of jealousy. The narratives of Jacob and Esau also depict sibling jealousy. Next comes the account of how the jealousy of Joseph's brothers resulted in their selling him into slavery. Living together is not easy. Most of us are intent on having things our way, and when that fails, we burn with envy, anger, and resentment. Often we get so consumed by thoughts of our own needs that we find it impossible to remember those of anyone else. We find the pages of Scripture littered with tales of those who attempted and failed to achieve community. But we should not abandon the quest for unity just because we find it difficult to achieve. Verse 2 gives us two beautiful poetic images.

Verse 2

"It is like precious oil poured on the head, running down on the beard, running down on Aaron's beard, down upon the collar of his robes."

Oil is a symbol of God's presence—an illustration of the Holy Spirit. Aaron was the first high priest, and Moses anointed him with oil when his brother took office. God chose Aaron, and God selected the manner by which he would come to office. Anointing with oil demonstrated that the blessing of God and the presence of the Holy Spirit lay upon Aaron. The oil used for anointing was a high-quality olive oil mixed with a blend of such things as cinnamon and myrrh. That means that as the oil ran down Aaron's head, not only was his head and body refreshed in that arid land, but the aroma refreshed his senses as well. All those who came near Aaron could smell the perfumed oil.

When the Holy Spirit is poured out on us, we become a source of refreshing to those around us. They sense the Spirit's presence in our lives, and that presence affects their lives as well.

God refreshed His servant Aaron with the oil of anointing. The psalmist uses the verb we translate as "running down" three times, thus indicating that the refreshing came from God. Repetition, in Hebrew, demonstrated that a thing was important or of extreme measure or quality. When the psalmist employed this verb three times he did so to indicate both the source and the quality of the blessing. This simple technique of the Hebrew literary style brings hope to people with broken lives. As sinners, we have been separated from God. But He has overcome our sin and brought harmony to our lives once again. He pours out blessings as fragrant oil running down our faces, onto our clothing, and covering the stench of our sin. Real community begins with the forgiveness of sins and restoration to fellowship with God. The Lord summons Christians to unite.

A man went to an asylum for the criminally insane. To his surprise, he discovered that only three guards at a time took care of 100 inmates. "Aren't you afraid that the inmates will unite, overcome you, and escape?" he asked one of the guards.

"Lunatics never unite," the guard replied.

COMMUNITY

But God has called us to something better, something higher. He has summoned us to genuine community. God makes such community a possibility through the reconciling atonement of Jesus and the blessings of the Holy Spirit. Because of those blessings, we can find true community with God and with fellow believers.

The Polish border town of Cieszyn has an interesting name. It's a contraction of a Polish sentence that means "I am happy." According to legend three brothers, long separated, were reunited in the place, and one said, "I am so happy," giving the town its name. This appears to be the spirit of Psalm 133. Happiness comes from reunion with God and with each other.

Community is essential for everyone who would know God. It is as refreshing as perfumed anointing oil running down over everyone who experiences God's great gift, affecting not only them but also those around who benefit from the aroma of Christian love and fellowship. The perfume of community draws others into fellowship, first with Jesus and next with those who love Him and enjoy relationship with Him.

History records that this was the way the first-century church grew. The political climate of the day did not allow much in the way of public meetings or public preaching, but the members of that early church took such care of one another that those on the outside saw their love for each other and asked how they could become a part of that kind of community. The fragrance of community drew them to the church. That's why Eugene Peterson writes, "Community . . . means people who have to learn how to care for each other."

According to a Gallup poll, four in 10 Americans admit to frequent feelings of intense loneliness. Don't you think that genuine community could do the same thing for the church and our cities today that it did 2,000 years ago? Genuine unity—community—acts as a magnet, attracting others. Biblical community also makes us strong and enables us to accomplish together what we could never do alone. When God's people experience community, they make beautiful music together to God's glory.

Sir John Barbirolli, an English conductor and cellist, held positions as conductor of the British National Opera Company and conductor of the New York Philharmonic Orchestra as well as several other prestigious positions. One time Barbirolli conducted an orchestra before a packed house on a Saturday night. The concert hall in which the orchestra was performing was used on Sundays for religious services. One of the patrons of the orchestra spotted in the audience the clergyman who was to preach there the next day. He went to the pastor and in a cynical tone said, "When are you going to fill this hall on Sunday the way Sir John Barbirolli has tonight?"

"I will fill this hall on Sunday morning," the minister replied, "when you give to me, as you gave to Sir John tonight, 85 disciplined men and women to be with him and to work with him." Community brings blessings to each individual believer, and it strengthens God's church to do its mission in this world. As we work together in community, we have power we could never before even imagine!

Around the beginning of the twentieth century a large plague of locusts swept over the states of Nebraska, Iowa, and Kansas. The locusts did more than $500 million worth of damage in just a few days. Now, that's $500 million in the currency of a century ago. How could insects do so much damage? They almost accomplished what none of our enemies could do at the time—wreck the nation's economy.

Locusts don't have a central government to organize them. Their army doesn't have a draft board. The insect simply knows it must be in community with other locusts. When locusts find community, they are able to overpower many things. If the locust knows it must have community, certainly beings as intelligent as we could learn this same lesson. It is in community that the Christian finds power. Verse 3 of Psalm 133 uses an interesting illustration of further benefits of community.

Verse 3
"It is as if the dew of Hermon were falling on Mount Zion. For there the Lord bestows his blessing, even life forevermore."

Mount Hermon is in the Anti-Lebanon Range just north of Israel. The highest mountain in that region, rising to more than 9,000 feet, it was proverbial for the dew and snow that fell on its slopes. If you've ever camped out at higher elevations, you know how heavy the dew can be. You wake up in the morning drenched. Mount Hermon's copious dew represents a sense of morning freshness and renewal for our spiritual lives.

As we gain a sense of expectancy that God will renew and bless us, we live in anticipation of what He will do next. What will God do today in your life—in my life? His Spirit renews us each morning, giving us endless possibilities for personal growth as well as for assisting Him in the birth of new believers. Such is the renewing power of God's Holy Spirit as symbolized by dew. Oil and dew. Oil flowing down Aaron's head and beard depicts healing and refreshing. The dew descending on Mount Hermon symbolizes a sense of freshness and newness. It gives us the right to expect that God will bring new growth to individuals and to our community. Oil and dew make community an experience of joy. Notice the last line of verse 3.

Verse 3
"For there the Lord bestows his blessing, even life forevermore."

What will heaven be like? What must it be like to live forever in that land of eternal bliss? The best hint we have of heaven we will find in the experience of community that Christ gives us here on earth. Revelation 4 and 5 give us a brief foreshadowing of heaven. And the best way to summarize what we discover there and in other related passages is that heaven will be a really good party! The best parties are the ones with the best people—people you love being with. They are those with whom we feel completely alive and from whom we receive the greatest joy. We can laugh with them, sometimes over "inside jokes," the ones only those who know each other really well can get. Many things do not need to be said, since a knowing look communicates as much as or more than words could ever say. When we do use words, our conversations are stimulating and yet at the same time comforting. They arise out of shared experiences and history and share emotions freely without judgment or condemnation. A few minutes with such friends can give us enough positive energy to last all week. If we can find just five minutes with people like that—five perfect minutes—then we are rich beyond measure. But heaven will be an eternity of such love and acceptance. "How good and pleasant it is when brothers live together in unity!" "The Lord bestows his blessing, even life forevermore."

This has not been easy for the church to achieve. Its history is littered with failures to achieve genuine community. One time that it did work, though, occurred during the first century. Luke, speaking of that church, writes that "they devoted themselves to the apostles' teaching and to the fellowship, to the breaking of bread and to prayer" (Acts 2:42).

On the day of Pentecost 120 people had gathered in the upper room, awaiting the direction of the Holy Spirit. When that Spirit drove them out into the streets to preach, they added 3,000 more that day. Jerusalem now had a church of 3,120 members! A church of that size had to have its problems. But several things kept them together.

First, "they devoted themselves to the apostles' teaching" (verse 42). Real community can establish itself only around a common set of biblically based teachings. We must be students of the Bible and come to an area of agreement in order to find true community.

Second, "they devoted themselves . . . to the breaking of bread" (verse 42). The church had a custom of eating meals together. Every day was a church potluck. They shared their food and other material possessions, giving generously to all who were in need. In short, they learned to care for each other.

Third, "they devoted themselves . . . to prayer (verse 42). Each believer had continual communion with God. They spent time in daily worship, in weekly corporate worship, and in constant prayer.

A part of what the verse implies is that they participated in the Lord's Supper together. That service reminds us of the fact that Jesus reconciled us to God by His sacrifice. It also reinforces the fact that the love of God reconciles us to each other. We need this. Let me suggest just a few ideas of how to attain true biblical community.

First, accept the reconciliation with God that Jesus won for us on Calvary's tree. Receive salvation as His free gift today.

Second, seek out a relationship with another committed believer, preferably of the same gender. It can be a prayer-partner relationship, an accountability relationship, or a mentoring relationship with someone more mature in the faith. Meet with this person on a regular basis.

Third, begin to have some level of participation in a small group of Christians who come together to study, pray, and support one another. This can be a vital step in the Christian life.

Fourth, form the habit of weekly worship at a Christ-centered, grace-oriented congregation. Test its doctrinal beliefs by the standard of Scripture, and then unite with them on a weekly basis.

Fifth, pray that God will teach us how to meet the needs of those in our circle of influence. Ask Him to give us a genuine love for people, and then request that He endow us with the strength to put that love into action. In this way we begin to satisfy our God hunger.

Andrew Murray wrote: "My relationship with God is part of my relationships with men. Failure in one will cause failure in the other." By the same token, success in one will lead to success in the other. We must make a commitment that we will pursue genuine community as a means of satisfying our hunger for God.

- ❖ If you are not yet a part of a biblical community, pray that God will lead you to unite with a church family that can serve as your community. Choose a congregation that makes Scripture central in their lives and teachings.
- ❖ Once you have become part of a church family, make it your practice to participate in the activities of that body of believers. This should include weekly attendance at worship services and midweek services. Join a small group, as well, that will provide Bible study, prayer, and times of personal sharing and mutual support.
- ❖ Learn what spiritual gifts God has given you and find opportunities to use them to build up your community of believers. Prayerfully volunteer your time for ministry in the church. Pray daily for your church family, asking God to give you a deeper love for each member.
- ❖ Work with other members of your church family to perform acts of kindness in the larger, unchurched community. Find ways together to communicate the love of Christ to others.
- ❖ When disagreements arise within the community, work quickly to resolve them amicably. Put aside all feelings of resentment and bitterness. Choose to love each other as Christ loves you.
- ❖ Covenant to pray daily in agreement with a prayer partner. Pray for a revival of true godliness in your church, and for the gospel to spread to the entire world in order that God might establish His kingdom among us.

CHAPTER 7

Meditation

(Psalm 77)

Remembering is a sacred act. Repeatedly Scripture calls us to do exactly that. Moses commands us to "remember the Sabbath day, to keep it holy" (Ex. 20:8, KJV). It was a weekly reminder that "the Lord made the heavens and the earth" (verse 11). Whenever Israel faced a new crisis, Moses, Joshua, David, or some other leader summoned the nation to think about God's past deliverance. Before they faced an uncertain future, Israel was called to remember a victorious past. God set the Passover as a remembrance of Israel's deliverance from Egypt. And before Joshua led the people into the Promised Land, he urged them to remember how God had delivered them from Pharaoh and then protected them during their sojourn through the wilderness. Scripture admonished young people to "remember your Creator in the days of your youth" (Eccl. 12:1). Jesus gave us emblems of water, bread, and wine, and told us to use them "in remembrance of me" (Luke 22:19).

The opposite of remembering is forgetting, and the Bible often encouraged God's people not to forget His many blessings. The Lord leads by example. When He urges us to remember and encourages us not to forget, He makes certain that we have a positive example to follow—His own. God tells us that He will not forget us; will not forget our names; will remember that we are weak, and therefore in need of help; and will remember us at the last day. With God, remembering is a sacred act.

Remembering is also a means of drawing nearer to God. As we remember, not only does it encourage us for today's difficulty, but it also reminds us of God's continual love for us. It reassures us that He has provided for our salvation—that He has made it possible for us to live without guilt and shame and that He will stop at nothing in order to provide for our reconciliation with Him. Remembering is a sacred act.

At times remembering can also be a cure for depression. In Psalm 77 Asaph is depressed. He pleads to God for help, and as he does, he remembers and is blessed.

Psalm 77:1, 2

"I cried out to God for help; I cried out to God to hear me. When I was in distress, I sought the Lord; at night I stretched out untiring hands and my soul refused to be comforted."

Most of us have felt like Asaph at some time. It appears to us that God has left us to suffer alone. Our prayers feel as though they bounce off the ceiling—no one, it seems, is listening. What makes it so difficult for Asaph is that he recollects a time that God was at work in his life and that of the nation. The Lord had once seemed very near. Their two hearts beat as one as God's hand revealed itself in every event of life.

Verse 3

"I remembered you, O God, and I groaned; I mused, and my spirit grew faint."

When Asaph remembers that God has been active, it fills him with pain. Our pain always increases when we lose what we once had. If we have never experienced a thing, we do not miss its absence as much as when we had it and it is now gone.

Destined for the Olympics, Jill Kinmont was a wonderful athlete, whom everyone said was a sure bet for a medal. The movie *The Other Side of the Mountain* tells how a skiing accident in 1955 changed her life forever. The accident left her paralyzed. Her fiancé was not able to cope with her paralysis, so he broke off the engagement. Jill had not only lost mobility and athletic skill but also the love of her life. As time passed, she found a new love, but he died in a plane crash. Her losses were so great that it made her grief unbearable. Jill had truly lost a lot, but that was only because she had had so much. At one time Jill had an athletic body and the opportunity to train and compete with it. She had had not just one but two great loves. You see, those who grieve greatly have loved greatly. If you have not loved, you do not grieve.

Asaph's pain is great only because his joy had been great. He has lost something very dear: the sense of God's active presence in his life. The pain, however, does not come just from his loss. The greatest pain results from

God's silence. Each hour that passes with no answer from God increases his pain. Why does God let things go on so long and so tragically? Why doesn't He give us at least a hint of His concern? Such divine silence causes excruciatingly painful suffering. Perhaps you know that pain. You may even be feeling it now. See if your heart doesn't resonate with Asaph's.

Verses 3-6

"I remembered you, O God, and I groaned; I mused, and my spirit grew faint. You kept my eyes from closing; I was too troubled to speak. I thought about the former days, the years of long ago; I remembered my songs in the night. My heart mused and my spirit inquired . . ."

What troubles Asaph most are his memories of the time he had been so happy. He had sung songs of joy before God—"songs in the night." The important word in this passage is "remembered." Here, he recalls his former happiness. Asaph feels sorry for himself, believing that God has been harsh with him. But the tone of the psalm changes with verse 7, and it is with that shift that he at last finds help.

Verses 7-9

"'Will the Lord reject forever? Will he never show his favor again? Has his unfailing love vanished forever? Has his promise failed for all time? Has God forgotten to be merciful? Has he in anger withheld his compassion?'"

Although Asaph declares in verse 1 that he is thinking about God, the truth is that his mind isn't on Him at all. He is focused on himself and his problems, and is indirectly blaming his anguish on God. As long as he engages in his little pity party, he cannot receive any help. In fact, the more he thinks about himself and his pain and God's supposed unfairness with him, the more he hurts. But when Asaph remembers God's "unfailing love," something changes. As he focuses more on God than on himself, he finds relief. Such relief comes when God becomes the center of our thoughts. However, notice how it is that Asaph begins to think about the Lord. He starts by questioning. At first it appears that he is interrogating the Lord Himself, but the questions are important in helping Asaph think more about God.

I have seen people react to tragedy in life with questions about God. They appear to be doubting their own faith, and that troubles many of those around them. But unless you examine your faith, you never truly own it. Questioning is usually a starting place for growth. Never fear the tough questions. Embrace them and submit them to clear thinking about God. Only then will true faith emerge and mature. Asaph asks about God, "Has his unfailing love vanished forever?"

Sometimes we miss nuances of a text because of the difficulties of translation. The question is something of a self-contradictory statement. The word translated as "unfailing love" is the Hebrew *hesed,* a word we studied in chapter 2. You will remember that it is so rich in its meaning that it requires 26 English words to capture it fully. It refers to a fanatical love that stops at nothing. Such love has fixated on the beloved, and it never ends. Asaph has other words he can choose to use for our word "love," but he selects *hesed.* I believe he does it on purpose. He uses it because it will be the answer to his question. God's love—His *hesed,* an undying love—never vanishes. We could translate Asaph's question as "Has God's indestructible love been destroyed?" If the love is indestructible, then it cannot be destroyed. Therefore, Asaph answers his own question within the question. No, God's love has not vanished, and it never will.

Granted, at times we feel as though God has removed His loving presence from us, but that perception is inaccurate. He never stops loving us. The apostle Paul asks, "Who shall separate us from the love of Christ? Shall trouble or hardship or persecution or famine or nakedness or danger or sword?" (Rom. 8:35).

Then he answers his own question. "No, in all these things we are more than conquerors through him who loved us. For I am convinced that neither death nor life, neither angels nor demons, neither the present nor the future, nor any powers, neither height nor depth, nor anything else in all creation, will be able to separate us from the love of God that is in Christ Jesus our Lord" (verses 37, 38).

God's love never vanishes, and when we remember this glorious truth, it will help us even in the midst of great trial and pain. Remembering God and His love and presence in our past will help draw each of us closer to Him. Remembering is a sacred act that establishes intimacy with the One who will never leave us or forsake us. Asaph then moves from questioning God to petitioning Him.

Verses 10-12

"Then I thought, 'To this I will appeal: the years of the right hand of the Most High.' I will remember the deeds of the Lord; yes, I will remember your miracles of long ago. I will meditate

on all your works and consider all your mighty deeds."

Asaph links two concepts together here. First, he says that he "will remember the deeds of the Lord; yes, I will remember your miracles." Then he promises to "meditate on all your works." He links the age-old practice of meditation to remembering, and implies that it is a means of satisfying our hunger for God.

Madame Guyon wrote: "Every Christian can elevate himself by meditation. . . . Silence in the presence of God, in which the soul, without being inactive, acts no longer except by divine impulse." Those who meditate may appear to be doing nothing, but the truth is that they are not inactive, but have simply refused to act unless God moves them to do so. They believe that activity not inspired by God is likely to be wrong activity. It would be better to wait until moved by God, and then respond in the full knowledge that what we do is in accordance with His will.

The best way to discover God's will is to focus on His previous blessings. Meditating on His works in our past prepares us to act in accordance with His will today.

Those who would draw near to God will remember His blessings in their lives, and will meditate on His deeds as well as on His character. Even in times of trial and pain, remembering His hand in our life can remind us that He will never leave nor forsake us, and that in His time He will again intervene in our behalf. Such remembering of our past history helps take the mind off self and place it on God.

"If we bring our minds back again and again to God," Paul Tournier wrote, "we shall be gradually giving the central place to God, not only in our inner selves, but in our practical everyday lives." God's solution for our dilemma is for us to focus our minds on Him. We are to bring to mind what He has done already, and as we do so, we can appeal to Him to again work in our behalf.

Verses 10–12

"Then I thought, 'To this I will appeal: the years of the right hand of the Most High.' I will remember the deeds of the Lord; yes, I will remember your miracles of long ago. I will meditate on all your works and consider all your mighty deeds."

Asaph appeals to God on the basis of memories of "miracles of long ago." He meditates on the Lord's mighty deeds.

Today many mistakenly link meditation with Eastern religions. However, biblical meditation predates such religions. God called us to meditate on Him and on His Word and His law long before such Eastern religions came into being. We see an example in Psalm 119, in which the psalmist states, "I meditate on your precepts and consider your ways" (verse 15).

Another example appears in Psalm 48. Here, instead of meditating on the law, or precepts, the psalmist dwells on an aspect of God's character. "Within your temple, O God, we meditate on your unfailing love" (verse 9). Remember, "unfailing love" is translated from the Hebrew *hesed*. It is a love so strong that the lover, God, cannot get the beloved, you and me, off His mind.

The psalmist said that he would meditate on this aspect of divine character. "Meditate" comes to us from a root word reminiscent of a cow chewing its cud. The cow eats green grass and swallows it. That grass goes to one of the cow's four stomachs for temporary storage. Later the cow brings that grass back into its mouth and chews it repeatedly before finally swallowing it. Meditation, then, is the process of bringing back to mind the Word of God, or an aspect of divine character, and going over it again and again.

William Grimshaw illustrated this when he wrote that meditation is the "soul's chewing." Such "chewing" can be done any time during the day. Many engage in this activity as they drive to and from work. Others prefer to find a time of quiet and a place of repose in order that they might focus the mind for meditation.

Another root form of the word "meditate" is used of a lion's soft growling over its freshly killed prey. Before the predator satisfies its hunger with the meat of the animal it has just killed, it growls, almost as if anticipating the pleasures of the meal ahead. As we apply this to meditation, it is sometimes helpful to quietly repeat a short portion of Scripture or a word describing an aspect of God's character. In doing so, we don't necessarily analyze the thing we are saying, but simply feel the fabric or texture of the word. We repeat it until it becomes a part of our being.

Richard Foster comments on the biblical words for meditation. "The Bible uses two different Hebrew words . . . to convey the idea of meditation, and together they are used some fifty-eight times. The words have various meanings: listening to God's word, reflecting on God's works, rehearsing God's deeds, ruminating on God's law, and more. In each case there is stress upon changed behavior as a result of our encounter with the living God."

Eastern religions encourage practitioners to make the mind blank for purposes of meditation. Biblical meditation encourages us to fill the mind with Scripture or with thoughts of God's character or mighty deeds. In so doing, we make Him the center of our attention instead of self or our problems. The Christian writer Brother Lawrence encouraged us to "think often on God, by day, by night, in your business, and even in your diversions. He is always near you and with you; leave Him not alone. You would think it rude to leave a friend alone who came to visit you; why, then, must God be neglected?"

Not only must He be the center of our attention; He is the focus of Christian meditation. We meditate on God in order that we might know Him, love Him, and serve Him. Again quoting Foster: "Christian meditation, very simply, is the ability to hear God's voice and obey His word."

Harvard University completed a study on the effect of meditation on older people. They discovered that it lowered blood pressure, improved mental function, and extended the life span. While such benefits are good news, the real purpose of meditation is to expand our experience with God. Deepening our worship, it brings a richer, fuller relationship with our Creator. It changes us, making us more and more like God.

Charles Swindoll observes that "the lost art of the twentieth century is meditation. Meditation is disciplined thought, forced on a single object or Scripture for a period of time." Every Christian should engage in some form of this practice. Someone once asked Dietrich Bonhoeffer, the German pastor martyred by the Nazis during World War II, why he meditated. "Because I am a Christian," Bonhoeffer replied. Meditation and Christianity should be synonymous. It is through this practice that we mine the depths of God. Turning the mind to Him and His interventions in our lives and in those of our ancestors provides healing for troubled souls. Asaph illustrates this.

Verses 13–15

"Your ways, O God, are holy. What god is so great as our God? You are the God who performs miracles; you display your power among the peoples. With your mighty arm you redeemed your people, the descendants of Jacob and Joseph."

What should we meditate on? Asaph suggests God's divine traits, His greatness, His miraculous intervention in human lives, and His redemptive work for the human race.

If you are new to the practice, may I make a few suggestions to help you get started?

MEDITATION

First, recognize your great need to engage in meditation. Our lives are frantic, constantly bombarded by messages that tend to detract from a holy life rather than contribute to it. Henry Wadsworth Longfellow penned: "The holiest of all holidays are those kept by ourselves in silence and apart: the secret anniversaries of the heart."

We desperately need the peace that arises from such times of contemplation. Having recognized our need, we then must set aside a specific time for meditation. Now, be careful here. Do not assume that meditation is something done only during specified times. It must also become a way of life. Paul tells us to "pray without ceasing" (1 Thess. 5:17, KJV). That means that God must be on our minds all day long. Continuously dwell on some portion of Scripture. That prepares us for our regular times of meditation. During them we must seek to experience what many have called "holy leisure." It is not a time of activity, but a period of quiet repose. Anyone who might observe us during such meditation might assume that we are doing absolutely nothing—simply wasting time. However, such "holy leisure" will equip us to handle the frantic, fragmented pace of life that we all experience in the twenty-first century.

Andrew Greeley commented that contemplation was a casualty of the American way of life, that Americans simply don't have time for it. America, he says, has so much leisure time that it has a leisure problem, and yet it lacks the essential leisure of contemplation.

Find a quiet place to engage in meditation. No telephones should be accessible, including your cell phone. We should permit no interruptions. It is helpful, but not absolutely necessary, if we are able to observe some natural beauty, such as a garden or trees or even some work of art. Choose a short passage of Scripture for meditation. Charles Haddon Spurgeon, the man referred to as the "Prince of Preachers," wrote: "I would rather lay my soul asoak in half a dozen verses [of the Bible] all day than rinse my hand in several chapters."

The psalms are excellent for this, as are the words of Jesus from the Gospels. Don't attempt to analyze the passage, but simply accept the words as you would those of a friend. Repeat them softly to yourself or silently in your mind. Many, however, have found it most helpful to say the words aloud in order that their texture, feel, and sound will register on their ears and mind. Don't be in a hurry to cover a lot of ground in the Bible. Bonhoeffer recommended spending a whole week on a single text! If you meditate on a story from the Gospels, seek to live the experience, applying all of your senses to the task. For example, smell the wheat fields, hear the wind blowing through the grain, taste the ripe kernels in the mouth, feel the sun on the back, see the crowd, and feel the longings in the heart. Live the story with all senses. Use the sanctified imagination, seeking to understand something of what it meant to be present at the time.

Alexander Whyte comments that "the truly Christian imagination never lets Jesus Christ out of her sight. . . . You open your New Testament. . . . And, by your imagination, that moment you are one of Christ's disciples on the spot, and are at His feet."

The goal is not so much to study the passage as it is to experience what the passage speaks to you. If it depicts peace, don't dissect the concept of peace, but just experience peace itself—enter into the reality of Christ's peace and become absorbed by it. Look at a biblical story from the standpoint of each of the characters engaged in the story. When meditating on the healing of the paralytic, see the story one day as the man who was paralyzed, the next day as one of the four friends who carried him on his bed to Jesus, another day as an observer in the crowd, and yet another as Jesus Himself. Experience the story from every angle until you are a part of it.

Close the time of "holy leisure" with a prayer of thanksgiving or commitment, or whatever else the Holy Spirit inspires you to pray. In this way Scripture becomes a part of your memory, an aspect of your reality. Experienced in this manner, the Bible changes our thoughts, beliefs, values, and behaviors. It becomes the living Word in us, all because we took the time to meditate, to contemplate, and to remember. Remembering is a sacred act.

Christian meditation allows us to relive memories of God's past involvement in our lives, as well as in those of all the believers who have existed before us. In so doing, the practice of meditation encourages us to look to the future, inspiring us to better deeds and better lives. I encourage you today, to set aside some time this week to practice biblical meditation. It is a marvelous means of satisfying your hunger for God.

EXERCISES:

Richard Foster says that "Christian meditation, very simply, is the ability to hear God's voice and obey His word." All of our activities in meditation seek these goals.

❖ Choose a passage of Scripture familiar to you, such as Psalm 23, to begin your meditations. It may be best to select only the first verse of the psalm to start with. Follow the steps suggested in this chapter to meditate on the passage.

❖ Set aside one hour per week to spend in some form of Christian meditation. Allow it to be a time of refreshing, renewal, and recreation for you.

❖ Find a place that is comfortable and quiet—a spot where nothing will interrupt you. Sit quietly for a few minutes, breathing deeply as you become aware of God's presence within you. Examine what is shaping your life today. Is there a particular joy that you are experiencing or a loss that you are grieving? Do you have an unanswered question in your life or a repressed emotion that needs to be expressed? What are the deepest longings of your heart? Do you desire more of God? When you become aware of those things in your life that need to be repaired, resist the urge to fix them. Feel the difference between doing something about it and just resting with it. What does it feel like to be still and let God work for you in this place of pain in your life?

Another form of meditation practiced by Christians during the Middle Ages was called "re-collecting." The Quakers have termed it "centering down." Again quoting Richard Foster in *Celebration of Discipline*:

"Begin by placing your palms down as a symbolic indication of your desire to turn over any concerns you may have to God. Inwardly you may pray, 'Lord, I give to You my anger toward John. I release my fear of my dentist appointment this morning. I surrender my anxiety over not having enough money to pay the bills this month. I release my frustration over trying to find a baby-sitter for tonight.' Whatever it is that weighs on your mind or is a concern to you, just say, 'palms down.' Release it. You may even feel a certain sense of release in your hands. After several moments of surrender, turn your palms up as a symbol of your desire to receive from the Lord. Perhaps you will pray silently: 'Lord, I would like to receive Your divine love for John, your peace about the dentist appointment, Your patience, Your joy.' Whatever your need, you say, 'palms up.' Having centered down, spend the remaining moments in complete silence. Do not ask for anything. Allow the Lord to commune with your spirits, to love you. If impressions or directions come, fine; if not, fine."

Such meditative activity may precede the kind of biblical meditation described in this chapter.

CHAPTER 8

Prayer

(Psalms 1; 2)

Eugene H. Peterson says that "prayer is answering language!" It is the language we use to respond to God. The Lord always speaks first. You have never prayed but what God has first called you to prayer. He placed in your heart the desire to pray. Your prayer was an answer to His initiative in your life. When God speaks, something happens in your heart. The Holy Spirit tells you that you need to respond to His leading in your life, and so you pray. It was not your idea to pray—it was God's. Prayer is never our initiative, but always God's. He always speaks first, and prayer is the language we use to answer Him. God is speaking to you today, just now, calling you to pray. It is time to answer Him. But it is difficult when you do not have the language.

Corrie ten Boom wrote about a little boy whose mother heard him reciting the alphabet while sitting in the corner of his room. "What are you doing?" she asked.

"Mom, you told me to pray," he replied, "but I have never prayed in my life, and I don't know how. So I gave God the whole alphabet and asked Him to make a good prayer of it."

Paraphrasing Eugene H. Peterson, we are unaccustomed to speaking with Deity and therefore, need instruction. Fortunately, the psalms give it to us.

The psalms are the tools that help us know how to answer God. Our mentors in the task of learning to respond to Him, they portray the great variety of work that He carries on in us. They address our rebellion and pain, as well as our trust and praise. God's gift to train us in prayer, they are our prayer masters. The psalms are examples of how to answer God

84

when He addresses us. Their purpose is primarily not to provide information about God, but to teach us how to live in intimacy with Him—how to speak with God when relating to Him personally. God speaks to us, and our answers are our prayers.

Donna was an avowed atheist. Because her parents were atheists as well, they had raised her to think that anyone who believed in the existence of God was a fool, incapable of rational thought. As an adult she became estranged from her father through some silly fight. In her anger she said some terrible things to her father. It had been six months since they had spoken to each other. Then Donna got the call from the hospital. Her parents had been involved in a terrible accident. Now her mother was dead and her father was barely clinging to life.

Quickly she raced to the hospital, hoping against hope that her father could hang on to life until she was able to reconcile with him. She ran into the ICU just in time to watch him breathe his last and die. Having lost both parents in one night and been robbed of the opportunity to reconcile with her father, she was devastated. As she drove home that evening, Donna wept. It was a stormy night with a heavy rain making it very difficult to see. The tears in her eyes didn't help either. The combination of bad weather and crying caused her to miss a turn and leave the road, nearly resulting in an accident of her own. Fortunately, she was able to bring the car safely to a stop.

Donna sat in the middle of a field with her heart racing and her eyes filled with the tears of grief over having lost both of her parents and not having been able to say that she was sorry to her father. In anger she banged her fist on the steering wheel and cried out, "Why, God? Why pick on me? I hate You."

To this day she swears that she heard an audible voice answer her. "Donna, that's the first time you've ever spoken to Me," it said, "and I just wanted to tell you that I love you."

God had moved in her life. He rewarded her first prayer, angry though it was, by speaking audibly. It was the first step to her eventual conversion.

The Lord always speaks first, and prayer is answering language. Our tendency is to talk about Him instead of talking to Him. The psalms teach us how to avoid this trap. If you would like to learn to pray, then you must pray the psalms. Don't pray them in order to understand your inner self, or to discover the meaning of life—pray, rather, in order that you might know and experience God. The psalms always make Him the center. You will not find the meaning of life when you pray the psalms—but you will find God.

The book of Psalms opens with two psalms that are not actually prayers themselves. Instead, they prepare us for prayer. Let's begin to learn to pray by reading Psalm 1.

Psalm 1

"Blessed is the man who does not walk in the counsel of the wicked or stand in the way of sinners or sit in the seat of mockers. But his delight is in the law of the Lord, and on his law he meditates day and night. He is like a tree planted by streams of water, which yields its fruit in season and whose leaf does not wither. Whatever he does prospers. Not so the wicked! They are like chaff that the wind blows away. Therefore the wicked will not stand in the judgment, nor sinners in the assembly of the righteous. For the Lord watches over the way of the righteous, but the way of the wicked will perish."

The psalms begin by telling us that those who are blessed will meditate on the law. Eugene H. Peterson notes that the word "law" in Scripture has a broader sense than just the Ten Commandments. Law can refer to all of the writings of Moses—in particular, the first five books of the Bible—as well as the Decalogue. Sometimes it can even include all of Scripture. The noun used for "law," here, comes from a verb that means to throw something like a javelin in such a way that it hits its target. When we meditate on the law, the words hit their mark and prepare us for prayer. God's Word is always accurately aimed. It is intentional and very personal. Scripture penetrates our defenses and cuts deeply into our hearts. There the words of Scripture do their work and communicate God's thoughts to us. They strike us where we live. Like laser-guided missiles, they find their target with deadly accuracy.

The psalmist tells us to meditate on the law. One aspect of meditation involves reciting the words. We are to say them aloud in order to get their feel and let them permeate us. This is different from just reading God's Word or thinking about it. We do not dissect the words or the sentences in order to understand the grammar or logic of thought. Like a cow chewing its cud, we simply taste the words and allow them to become a part of us. Verse 3 tells us that whoever meditates on God's Word becomes like "a tree planted by streams of water."

God's people collected and organized the psalms during the Babylonian captivity. They had been exiled to a flat and arid country. A single river flowed through Babylon. But its inhabitants had excavated a network of irrigation canals in order to provide water for agriculture. The Israelites worked in the fields watered by those canals. Homesick and discouraged, they assumed that as long as they were living in captivity they could not pray. "How shall we sing the Lord's song in a strange land?" they asked themselves (Ps. 137:4, KJV).

But they did learn to pray and sing in that distant country. They did it through the practice of meditation. The Israelites meditated on God's Word, and became like that tree planted by the irrigation canal. They put down roots, sent out leaves, and produced fruit. Before they knew it, they were praying and singing the Lord's song in a foreign land.

What kind of tree do you think of when you read this psalm?

I grew up in Texas, and so one of the trees I know best is the mesquite. Mesquite trees are not very tall, don't give much shade, and are not of any particular use except that people say that it is a good wood to use when cooking certain foods over an open fire. But I don't think that a mesquite tree is what the psalmist had in mind here. I believe he thought of a great cedar, or a mighty oak, or some wonderful fruit tree. None of them would survive very well in the desert of Iraq, but when planted beside an irrigation ditch, they would have the opportunity to flourish even in that hot country.

Often people believe that they could pray better if their circumstances would change. If they could live in a different city or if they had a different job or a different spouse, then they could pray. The psalmist tells us that your circumstances will not keep you from prayer. You can be like a tree in Babylon, planted next to an irrigation ditch. Even there you will be able to sink your roots deep into the earth through the practice of meditation on Scripture.

Most horticulturalists would tell you that Babylon is not the ideal place to plant a fruit tree. The land is too hot, too arid, and too devoid of the nutrients needed to produce good fruit. But when planted next to an irrigation ditch, fruit trees can survive and bear good fruit. The psalmist is telling us that if we really want to learn to pray and if we have been putting that experience off until our circumstances improve, we need only look at a tree to convince ourselves otherwise.

Eugene Peterson reminds us that another thing we can learn from a careful study of a tree is this: prayer begins with what we see. It starts with the realities of your life, not with esoteric concepts. Prayer incorporates your life, your pain, your hardships, and your struggles. Meditating on Scripture focuses the attention on things that matter to you, and therefore that also matter to God.

Max Lucado has shared the story of a dying man in a hospital, who, a few days before his death, had a visit from a minister. Next to the man's bed was an empty chair. The minister, noticing it, asked if somebody had also recently stopped by to see him. The old man smiled and said, "I place Jesus on that chair and I talk to him." Then he went on to explain. "Years ago a friend told me that prayer was as simple as talking to a good friend. So every day I pull up a chair, invite Jesus to sit, and we have a good talk."

Several days later the man died. His daughter had been away from his room, and when she returned, she found that her father had died. Strangely, though, his head was not resting on his pillow, but on an empty chair beside his bed. It wasn't until the minister shared his conversation with her that she understood. Her father recognized that very few things actually mattered. But answering God does, and prayer is the method by which we do that.

Three men were discussing the proper posture for prayer. The first said that a person should be on knees with head bowed in reverence to the Almighty. The second argued that one should stand with head raised looking into the heavens and speak into the face of God as a little child. The third spoke up and said, "I know nothing about these positions, but I do know this: the finest praying I've ever done was while hanging by my feet, upside down, in a well!"

Psalm 2 tells us that when things go wrong, or it appears that our enemies want to destroy us, prayer is an active means of changing things.

Psalm 2:1-6

"Why do the nations conspire and the peoples plot in vain? The kings of the earth take their stand and the rulers gather together against the Lord and against his Anointed One. 'Let us break their chains,' they say, 'and throw off their fetters.'

"The One enthroned in heaven laughs; the Lord scoffs at them. Then he rebukes them in his anger and terrifies them in his wrath, saying, 'I have installed my King on Zion, my holy hill!'"

The verb translated "meditate" in Psalm 1 is rendered as "plot" in verse 1 of Psalm 2.

Verse 1

"Why do the nations conspire and the peoples plot in vain?"

To meditate, when using this verb, is to ruminate over the Word of God. Psalm 1 employs it to suggest that our lives are enriched as we med-

88

itate on Scripture. But Psalm 2 uses the same verb negatively. Here it describes people who plot against God, His Word, and His people. They are devising schemes against Him in order to thwart His will in their lives and the lives of others. Having rejected the sovereignty of God in their lives, they now seek to put themselves in control.

Verse 2 tells us that such individuals are willing to use force to achieve their goals.

Verse 2

"The kings of the earth take their stand and the rulers gather together against the Lord and against his Anointed One."

What are Christians to do in such circumstances? What are we to do when people actively, intentionally, conspire to defeat God's plans in the world? Psalm 1 encourages us to meditate on God's Word, and tells us that when we do that, we are like a tree.

Who would you bet would be more likely to win such a confrontation: Bible-meditating trees or the kings and rulers of the world? Many Christians have concluded that they have no chance against such "superior" forces. It is easy for them to be intimidated into standing by idly as earthly powers have their way. Prayer, however, is designed to unleash God's activity in the world. We spend so much time gazing on the strength of the enemy that we forget God and His mighty power. Our attention must instead focus on God.

A young lieutenant was hosting a four-star general. While they were in the subordinate's office, the phone rang, and he instinctively reached over to answer it. The general intercepted the young man's hand and said, "You don't need to answer it. Whoever it is, they can't be more important than I am."

God far outranks everyone else and is therefore worthy of our undivided attention. In fact, He is not too worried about the bullies of the world, even when they combine their considerable forces against Him and His people. God's response to their attempted intimidation is somewhat surprising.

Verses 4-6

"The One enthroned in heaven laughs; the Lord scoffs at them. Then he rebukes them in his anger and terrifies them in his wrath, saying, 'I have installed my King on Zion, my holy hill.'"

We tremble before the armies of this earth, feel small when confronted with their judiciaries and legislatures, and cower with fear as we face the possibilities of punishment or even execution. While we might consider ourselves helpless against their wrath, we must remember that all true power resides not in the forces of this world, but in heaven with our omnipotent God. When we pray, we access to that power as we align ourselves with the center of the entire universe. Prayer enables us to see that God is truly in control. It opens our eyes to the immensity of His might—His limitless power and reign.

Psalm 2 presents this by introducing the Messiah, God on earth. Jesus invaded our planet and neutralized the power of its rulers. Jesus dealt a devastating blow right to the solar plexus of the strongman who stands against us. Meditating on Scripture enables us to see that Jesus is the one who will take action against the enemies of heaven. It is a battle that we will not need to fight.

Verse 6
"I have installed my King on Zion, my holy hill."
Because of what Jesus accomplished when He invaded earth, God laughs at the pseudopowers that seek to destroy His people and block His reign on this earth. His laughter is good news for His people. When He laughs, His people can rest. His laughter grants us proper perspective. Why should we take seriously those at whom He laughs? God is much too strong for them.

Just the other day I was praying about a problem that I'm facing. It seems to me that angry forces are gathering their strength to hurt God's work. I worried about it for some time, and then I remembered Psalm 2. Praying just one prayer, I simply asked God to look at this situation that seemed so hopeless to me, and laugh. When He does, the problem is solved. And when He laughs, we can rest with ease, for our God is in control. The incredible thing is this—God has ordained that the soldiers in His army should defeat the powerful of this world through meditating on Scripture and praying Scripture. When we do that, He laughs at our enemies, and we become invincible.

Verses 8, 9
"Ask of me, and I will make the nations your inheritance, the ends of the earth your possession. You will rule them with an iron scepter; you will dash them to pieces like pottery."
God has ordained that His Bible-meditating people should rule over the

wicked powers of our world. Why should we fear? The God we pray to is more powerful than the enemies we fear. As Max Lucado has written: "The power of prayer is not in the one who prays but in the one who hears it." God calls us to serve Him through another type of prayer, adoration.

Verse 11
"Serve the Lord with fear and rejoice with trembling."

Not only does God call His people to pray the prayer of adoration, but He also summons the rulers of the earth to do the same.

Verse 10
"Therefore, you kings, be wise; be warned."

God establishes His sovereignty on earth through His praying people. As His people worship, adore, meditate, and pray, it confirms His reign. Psalm 2 reminds us of His omnipotence, and this prepares us for prayer. Both Psalms 1 and 2 direct us to Scripture and focus our attention on God's rulership of all.

When we read and pray Psalm 1, we become trees that draw the water and nutrients of Scripture as we meditate on God's Word. We listen as He speaks and prepare to answer as He initiates the conversation.

Psalm 2 enables us to recognize that God's power dwarfs that of the wickedness of this world. It rivets our attention on Him and His divine authority. All of this is vital. More than anything else, it is the true work of Christians. It may feel as if we are wasting time, but it is essential that we wait until God directs our activities.

Eugene Peterson wrote that "in prayer, we are aware that God is in action and that when the circumstances are ready, when others are in the right place, and when our hearts are prepared, He will call us into action. Waiting in prayer is a disciplined refusal to act before God acts."

Look at the great names from church history, and you will discover that the more esteemed the name, the stronger the prayer life. Consider just a few examples.

Charles Haddon Spurgeon, the man known as "the Prince of Preachers," wrote, "As artists give themselves to their models, and poets to their classical pursuits, so must we addict ourselves to prayer."

Martin Luther, that great figure of the Reformation, was also a man of prayer. He observed that "as it is the business of tailors to make clothes and of cobblers to mend shoes, so it is the business of Christians to pray." To those too busy to pray, Luther said, "I have so much business I cannot get on without spending three hours daily in prayer."

Nineteenth- and early twentieth-century Christian writer Ellen White wrote that "prayer is the breath of the soul." If true, is it any wonder that the spiritual life of so many professed Christians appears to be dead? Their souls have asphyxiated!

Ralph Waldo Emerson called prayer "the contemplation of the facts of life from the highest point of view."

John Wesley devoted himself to two hours of prayer every day. He declared that "God does nothing but in answer to prayer."

Oswald Chambers, whose writings have blessed so many throughout the years, emphasized the importance of prayer for the Christian when he declared that "prayer does not equip us for greater works—prayer is the greater work."

Raymond McHenry took that a step further when he suggested, "May we never experience success without prayer."

Bible commentator William Barclay wrote: "Prayer is not flight; prayer is power. Prayer does not deliver a man from some terrible situation; prayer enables a man to face and to master the situation."

If time and space allowed, we could cite many, many more great champions of faith who spoke of the importance of a life devoted to prayer. Their testimony tells us that the journey to God begins on our knees, in prayer.

I have struggled with prayer all my life. My personality is such that I prefer to be active rather than in waiting on God in prayer, a tendency that has brought me more pain than even I know. But every time I devote myself to prayer, God opens Himself to me, and my life is changed as my ministry becomes more productive and my spiritual journey filled with greater joy. My struggle is to wait for God to move and then to respond to his voice. When that happens, He leads me in paths of obedience. Not only am I blessed by this, but those around me as well.

Tony Campolo is a well-known Christian author and communicator. Once when he arrived on the campus of a college to speak for the chapel service, his host first escorted him to a back room where eight men laid their hands on him and began to pray. Campolo said he was very appreciative of the heartfelt prayers, but one individual spent a long time praying about something that had nothing to do with the chapel service. The guy prayed on and on about a friend of his named Charlie.

"God, you know Charlie," the man said. "He lives in that silver trailer down the road about a mile. You know the trailer, Lord, just down the road on the right-hand side."

Campolo began to think to himself, *Knock it off, buddy. God knows where this guy lives.*

"Lord, Charlie told me this morning he's decided to leave his wife and three kids," the man went on. "He's going to walk out on his family. Lord, step in, do something, bring that family together again." To Campolo's growing frustration, the guy just kept praying earnestly for his friend Charlie, and kept reiterating the fact that the man was leaving his wife and three kids and that he lived in a silver trailer, just down the road on the right-hand side.

By now Campolo had grown weary and couldn't wait for the prayer to end. Finally it did, and he went in to preach for the chapel service. Afterward, Campolo got into his car and started heading home. Soon thereafter, he saw a hitchhiker and pulled over to give him a ride. As they pulled back onto the road, Campolo introduced himself, and the hitchhiker said his name was Charlie. Campolo's heart began to race, and he took the next exit off the turnpike. The passenger asked him why he was exiting, and Campolo said, "Because you just left your wife and three children, right?"

The man's eyes got real big and he said, "R-r-r-ight." He leaned closer to the door and never took his eyes off Campolo. Imagine what he thought when Campolo drove him right to his silver trailer.

"How'd you know I live here?" Charlie asked.

"God told me," Campolo replied. Then he ordered Charlie to return to the trailer.

The man hurried to the door, where his wife met him at the doorway and shouted, "You're back, you're back!" The husband then whispered in her ear and her eyes grew bigger and bigger.

By then Campolo had come up to the porch. "Sit down," he said. "I'm going to talk, and the two of you are going to listen." It was the most captive audience he had ever addressed. That afternoon those two people were led to Jesus Christ, and today Charlie is a preacher of the gospel.

Prayer begins when we listen to God, who always speaks first. As we meditate on Scripture, He prepares us to reply to His voice. Since God is sovereign, we need not fear any enemy, for God simply laughs at their pretense of power. And when, finally, we respond, the results can be simply amazing.

Listen! God is calling you to prayer today.

EXERCISES:

Often those who are new in Christ experience prayer that is filled with words. Like new lovers who cannot wait to tell their beloved everything about themselves, a new believer pours out a flood of words to God in prayer. This time of wordiness is often followed by one of deeper study in which the person learns doctrine and gains greater information about God. This new knowledge often leads to prayers of praise and thanksgiving for their new understanding of who God is and what He does.

Eventually, though, most believers come to a point at which their prayers feel empty, dry, and repetitive. They may find themselves with nothing to say, or certainly, nothing of real interest or intensity of emotion. Feelings of guilt or inadequacy usually accompany such times.

What they need now in their spiritual life is fewer words. Scripture speaks of "groanings" too deep for words. Many have said that the best prayers often have more groans than words. That is because the dryness in the prayer life of a more mature believer is actually God's invitation to a deeper form or prayer—a prayer of fewer words and deeper intensity.

Have you noticed how couples who have been married a great many years can often know what the other is feeling or thinking without being told? A glance, a gesture, or a sigh can communicate more than 1,000 words shared between partners in a new marriage. Mature couples are often comfortable just being with their partner without saying much and yet knowing that this is just fine. Such a relationship doesn't happen overnight. It takes years of intimacy to develop.

Perhaps this is the type of intimate relationship the mature believer's time of dryness in prayer is calling us to experience. Maybe God is summoning you to an experience of silent prayer, a prayer without words. This is a call to deeper intimacy with Him.

One way to experience this deeper intimacy of a prayer without words is called "prayer breath." Prayer breath begins with acknowledging that we do not know how to pray, but that only the Holy Spirit can pray. We ask the Spirit to give us a word of prayer, one that expresses our greatest need.

Ask yourself what your greatest longing might be. Request the Spirit to reveal it to you. Find a way to express that longing in just six to 10 syllables. For me recently my prayer breath has been, "Lord, make me long for more of You."

At other times your prayer breath may be the thing you most know to be true about God. It could be something like "Lord Jesus, You are life to me."

Some have chosen to pray, "Lord Jesus Christ, have mercy on me, a sinner."

Once you have chosen your prayer breath, use it as you breathe in and out. As you drive your car in traffic, simply repeat your prayer breath again and again. As you stand in line or as you sit at your desk, allow this prayer to cycle through your mind repeatedly. Pray it when you are worried or anxious, or when you need some assurance of God's presence. This enables you to pray without ceasing. It becomes the life breath of your prayer life.

Use your prayer breath until you feel it is no longer your deepest longing. Then chose another prayer breath and employ it in the same manner. You will find that this prayer will open the door to a deeper awareness of God's presence in your life.

Here are some more activities for a deeper prayer life.

- ❖ Choose specific times of the day for prayer. D. L. Moody said that prayer must be brief, intense, and frequent. Such a pattern is best for some, especially those who would classify themselves as beginners. Mark times for prayer on your Palm Pilot or Day Planner. Treat them as important appointments.

- ❖ God is calling you to pray, but you, being mortal, do not have the right words to use to answer God. It can be helpful to borrow the prayers of Scripture. Choose a prayer you find in the Bible, such as one of the psalms or one of Paul's great prayers or even Jesus' prayer in John 17, and employ it as your own. Change personal pronouns and other words as necessary in order to make it more relevant to your life. Repeat the prayer several times, and then sit in silence. Wait for God to speak to you. If He says nothing, fine. If He impresses you with something, then make the appropriate response. Repeat this daily for a week.

- ❖ The ancients used to pray five psalms each day, thus going through the entire psalter within a month. They repeated the process 12 times each year. If five psalms a day seems a bit ambitious for you, then start with one a day. As you pray, notice the raw honesty and openness of such prayers. Take note of patterns and of the author's focus in each psalm. Look for emotions, thoughts, and conflict. What can you learn from this? Use the psalms as a pattern for your prayer life.

- ❖ Write or type your prayers. Many people find that this helps them organize their thoughts and keeps them on track.

❖ Experiment with different patterns of prayer, such as the ACTS pattern. A stands for adoration, C for confession, T for thanksgiving, and S for supplication. Don't be afraid to change patterns or methods.

❖ Keep a prayer list with names of people, specific problems or concerns, government officials, and institutions you want to pray for. Keep a record of answered prayers as well. Give thanks for answers to prayers.

❖ Try another method of praying without words. Visualize God in a majestic setting. See yourself in adoration, praise, and worship. Visualize a line of people standing nearby—the people for whom you have been praying. Then imagine yourself taking each of them, one by one, to God, and watch as He enfolds each in His arms. God meets their every need and makes everyone completely whole. After the last person on your list has come before God, it is now your turn. Visualize His embrace, feel His warmth and power, and experience the satisfaction of your every need. Don't be afraid to sit in silence during any prayer. Just enjoy being in God's presence.

❖ Use scriptural promises in prayer. Cite them before God and claim the fulfillment of each promise for yourself and for others.

❖ Pray weekly with a prayer partner. Agree to pray for specific items during your sessions. While the first partner presents a brief prayer, the other partner should listen and build upon the previous prayer. Take turns praying in this manner, with each expanding on the previous prayer. If one brings up a particular concern, let the other add an "amen" to that concern and perhaps even delve more deeply into the matter. Encourage one another to pray daily while you are apart from one another.

❖ Understand that there is no wrong way to pray. The only wrong thing to do in prayer is to fail to pray. Make prayer a part of your daily experience. Pray while driving, while washing clothes or dishes, while mowing the lawn, or while performing any other menial task. Pray at all times.

CHAPTER 9

Generosity and Trust

(Psalm 49)

Where do you place your trust?
On the day before Easter, April 18, 1992, in Austin, Texas, Madalyn Murray O'Hair kicked off the twenty-second Annual National American Convention of Atheists. In her opening remarks she said, "As long as there is religious slavery, mental slavery, we're not going to get anywhere as a nation. So we're calling for the total, complete, and absolute elimination of religion in American culture. We would not be in difficulty [as a nation] if we weren't being ruled by those classes of persons who believe in fantasy."

O'Hair declared that they were holding the convention of atheists on Easter weekend because "we want to take back Easter and make it a celebration of the start of spring." As participants at the convention marched on the state capitol, one atheist held a placard that stated: "In God We Trust. Not!" Remember that practice of negating a positive statement by adding "not" on the end that was especially popular a few years ago? Atheists tell us that they do not place their trust in God.

Do you trust in God? Where do you place your trust?

We have been studying the psalms in order that we might discover how to satisfy our hunger for God. Psalm 49 tells us that one of the things we can do to fulfill us spiritually is to learn to trust God by becoming generous people.

Psalm 49:1-4
"Hear this, all you peoples; listen, all who live in this world, both low and high, rich and poor alike: My mouth will speak

words of wisdom; the utterance from my heart will give understanding. I will turn my ear to a proverb; with the harp I will expound my riddle."

The beginning of this psalm sounds more like something from the book of Proverbs than Psalms. It is a psalm of instruction, and the lesson it gives is this: riches are empty. A message applicable to rich and poor alike, it goes to the rich since they may trust their money rather than God. And it is given to the poor in order to ensure that they do not long for the empty promise of security offered by money. Instead, all should long for God and the wonderful security He alone offers to all who trust in Him.

In verse 3 the psalmist says that he is offering "words of wisdom" that he claims will "give understanding." The words "wisdom" and "understanding" are both plural in the Hebrew. The biblical author chose the plural form of the nouns to emphasize the importance of what he had to say. Furthermore, he claims to have solved a "riddle." What is the riddle? Let's read on.

Verses 5-9

"Why should I fear when evil days come, when wicked deceivers surround me—those who trust in their wealth and boast of their great riches? No man can redeem the life of another or give to God a ransom for him—the ransom for a life is costly, no payment is ever enough—that he should live on forever and not see decay."

The psalmist here speaks of a reoccurring practice down through the ages. Some people have gained their fortune on the backs of the poor. Obviously, not all the rich are this way. Abraham and Job are examples of rich individuals who did not gain wealth by taking advantage of the poor. However, others have oppressed the less advantaged.

The psalmist assures us that we have nothing to fear from those who value money above people. He tells us that those who trust in wealth are actually foolish. Money cannot save a person from death. The rich and poor alike die. Our focus should be not on gaining wealth but on securing heaven.

Verse 7

"No man can redeem the life of another or give to God a ransom for him."

That means that money cannot buy life. Even the wealthiest people on earth cannot pool their funds and come up with enough to buy more life for someone or to redeem it. Money cannot ensure that we will not die. To think otherwise is foolish.

Verse 10

"For all can see that wise men die; the foolish and the sense- less alike perish and leave their wealth to others."

Death comes to all, and when it does, you cannot take anything with you. I've never seen a hearse pulling a trailer, have you?

When I was a young man, I traveled with a Christian singing group. On one occasion I neglected to pack a suit. I had a clean shirt and tie, socks and shoes, but no suit. I explained my plight to the local pastor, who im- mediately called one of his members. The man was a funeral director. The mortician asked what my size was and brought one of the suits he kept for burying people who did not own a suit. The suit had been especially made for this very purpose. I quickly put it on before our concert.

The suit fit quite nicely, but I noticed one peculiarity. It had no pock- ets! What need does a corpse have for pockets?

We are all going to die, and when it happens, we cannot take anything with us. The psalmist says that everyone can see this obvious fact. But while they can, some still will not accept it. They refuse to admit that they might possibly die.

Charles Spurgeon told the story of a wealthy man in Massachusetts whose passion was to buy land. He bought all the property surrounding his own farm. However, the owner of one small farm right in the middle of his vast holdings refused to sell. The owner was very poor, but held on to his land.

One day the rich man learned that the poor man was in financial trou- ble. It appeared as though he would probably lose his meager farm.

Although the wealthy man eagerly waited to buy the land when it be- came available, the poor man managed to surprise everyone by meeting all his obligations and paying off the entire debt. It greatly upset the rich man. Determined to get that piece of property, he declared, "My neighbor is an old man. He cannot live long, and when he is dead I will buy the lot." The irony is that the poor neighbor was 58, and the wealthy man was 60! This man refused to admit the obvious fact that one day he would die. He ac- knowledged that his "elderly" neighbor was sure to die, but not he.

The psalmist continues his thoughts about the inevitable deaths of both the rich and poor, and the wise and the foolish, in verses 11 and 12.

Verses 11, 12

"Their tombs will remain their houses forever, their dwellings for endless generations, though they had named lands after themselves. But man, despite his riches, does not endure; he is like the beasts that perish."

If we do not gain a basic understanding of true wealth, we live just like animals. And it has devastating consequences. Verse 12 says that such a person "does not endure." The literal translation of the Hebrew is that he "does not pass the night." It tells us that our lives are so tenuous that we have no assurance that we will wake up in the morning. Those who fail to understand the true value of money and that of true riches are doomed to the same fate as the animals.

Years ago a monk saw a man in desperate need. Traveling, the person had lost his money to thieves. The monk opened his small pouch of belongings and offered the man a precious stone worth a small fortune. The monk had not purchased the stone, but had found it, and now he was willing to give it away to someone in need. Amazed at his good fortune, the robbery victim quickly left to sell the valuable gem. A few days later, however, he returned, still holding the jewel. Placing it in the monk's hand, he said, "Now, please give me something much more precious than this. Please give me that which enabled you to give it away."

The man realized that something had even greater value than money. The monk knew the secret, and the traveler desired to have it more than he did the wealth he could possess by selling the gemstone.

And what was the secret? Simply this. The wise refuse to put their faith in riches. Instead, they place their trust in God. And as they do, they find that God changes their attitudes toward money, and He transforms their attitudes toward people. Instead of hoarding wealth, they become generous. But it all starts by establishing trust in that which truly matters. It commences by trusting in God and not in money.

John D. Rockefeller achieved what our culture calls success by amassing more wealth than he could ever spend. By the time he was 53 his life was a wreck. His wealth did not bring him security. In fact, the businessman once commented, "I never placed my head upon the pillow at night without reminding myself that my success might only be temporary." Although he was the richest man in the world, he was still miserable in every sense of the word. He was sick physically, mentally, and emotionally. His life had no humor, balance, or joy.

Then a transformation occurred. Determined to become a giver rather than an accumulator, Rockefeller began to give his millions away. He founded the Rockefeller Foundation, which donated money to fight disease and ignorance. Living to be 98, he became a happy man during his later years because of his new and revitalized definition of success. John D. Rockefeller learned that those who trust in money are fools.

The Christian attitude toward money is not a hostile one, but an attitude formed by a correct understanding of its proper use and its limitations. Psalm 49 teaches us that we cannot place our confidence in wealth. The psalmist compares those who trust in money to sheep awaiting slaughter.

Verses 13, 14

"This is the fate of those who trust in themselves, and of their followers, who approve their sayings. Like sheep they are destined for the grave, and death will feed on them. The upright will rule over them in the morning; their forms will decay in the grave, far from their princely mansions."

Sheep who await slaughter have no idea what confronts them. They are dumb animals, marching inexorably to certain death. Those who trust in wealth are no different. By the way, you don't have to be wealthy to fit into this category. I've seen minimum-wage earners who put their confidence in their weekly check. They didn't have much money, but they trusted in what they had. They, too, were like sheep heading for slaughter.

Contrast this scene with a picture of those who trust in God.

Verse 15

"But God will redeem my life from the grave; he will surely take me to himself."

Earlier the psalmist declared that no one was rich enough to redeem anyone's life or to extend and add to it. God alone has the ability to redeem a life from the grave. Certainly it is better to trust in Him than in money. Money is here today and, very often, gone tomorrow. Your salary could disappear at any moment. In an age of corporate downsizing, no one is safe—nothing is secure.

If you trust in such things as your job or your savings, you are as foolish as sheep penned up for slaughter. But if your trust is in God, your life will be redeemed. Those who put their confidence in riches will die, be buried, and be forgotten, but those who trust in God will be redeemed by Him, and will then spend eternity with Him.

The psalmist closes his discourse on money by making an appeal to wisdom.

Verses 16-20

"Do not be overawed when a man grows rich, when the splendor of his house increases; for he will take nothing with him when he dies, his splendor will not descend with him. Though while he lived he counted himself blessed—and men praise you when you prosper—he will join the generation of his fathers, who will never see the light of life. A man who has riches without understanding is like the beasts that perish."

Wealth is temporary and limited. Jesus is eternal and limitless. The contrast couldn't be greater. Our trust must be in God. When we place our trust in Him, He changes our attitudes about money. We then see it as a gift from God, something to use for His purposes.

While the psalmist does not condemn those who have money, he does chastise those who have money but no understanding. Look again at verse 20.

Verse 20

"A man who has riches without understanding is like the beasts that perish."

I have friends who have been blessed with money and with understanding. They recognize that wealth is a gift, but not one to be trusted. Instead, they use their money as a means of blessing others. I have seen such friends seek out people whose lives are in distress and offer to help. They have money and understanding, and that makes all the difference.

William Barclay wrote that "the finest gifts are given, not after waiting until need has to ask, but by the person whose eye sees, whose heart feels, and whose hand is stretched out even before any request is made." I have been blessed to be able to watch people who live this way.

This brings us back to the main focus of our study in the book of Psalms. We have been seeking ways to satisfy our hunger for God. A proper understanding and use of money can assist us in that search.

How should we view money? May I suggest just a few ways?

First, all things, including money, belong to God and come from Him. We are merely stewards of the things that He has entrusted to our care. The rightful owner of everything, He declares, "The silver is mine and the gold is mine" (Haggai 2:8). That means that everything you have in your bank account, all the real estate you own, and all your stocks and bonds, belong to Him, and came to you directly from God. This is the first and most important understanding to have about money: God is the owner, and we are merely stewards.

Among other things, this teaches us to trust in Him rather than self. It makes us recognize His sovereignty and power as contrasted with our own weakness.

Second, money is temporary and extremely limited. It comes and it goes. You can lose what you have very easily, so we should always view wealth as fleeting. And it is limited in that it cannot buy you happiness, meaning and purpose, or even life itself. The psalmist reminded us that:

Verses 7, 8
"No man can redeem the life of another or give to God a ransom for him—the ransom for a life is costly, no payment is ever enough."
Money cannot purchase life, love, or happiness. Even the Beatles used to sing that it can't buy you love. Thus money is temporary and limited in what it can do.

Third, God gives us money to meet our own necessities, advance the mission of the gospel, care for others, and enjoy our life with. God does want us to be able to provide for housing, food, clothing, educating our children, and even retirement. Money is His gift to us to enable us to fulfill those requirements.

The Lord also wants us to use money to advance the spread of the gospel. To that end, He established the system of tithes and offerings for the purpose of supporting the church and evangelizing the entire world. It is a privilege to participate in this work by returning a faithful tithe and by the giving of love offerings to God.

Mary Magdalene is an example of someone who presented an offering to Jesus out of a heart filled with love for her Savior. She spent an amount equivalent to a laborer's yearly wage to buy a bottle of perfume to anoint Jesus. It was a gift of love and thereby serves as an example for all of us.

In addition to our gifts to the church, we are also to stand ready to help others. Scripture informs us that the earliest church had no needy people in it. How could this be? Were they just very selective in whom they allowed into membership? No, the members used their own resources to meet the needs of fellow believers. That is how Scripture could say that there were no needy people among them.

But money is also something God meant to be enjoyed. It is not wrong to enjoy it any more than it is wrong to enjoy sunshine, fresh air, good food, and love. All are gifts from God's hands and meant for our pleasure. Money falls into this same category. As long as we are certain to put the needs of the gospel and the needs of others before our own enjoyment, it is not wrong to appreciate the bounty that God has supplied.

Although money has limitations, it does have some power. One of the places we see its impact is in the realm of debt. When you owe money, the person you owe it to has control over your life. Perhaps that is why Scripture admonishes us to be neither lender nor borrower. We are the slave of the person we owe money to, so avoiding debt is a better way to live. If we have these understandings in mind, then when God does give money to us, we will trust not in it, but in the One who bestows the money on us.

Eleven-year-old Ryan Rigney, of Manchester, Tennessee, decided that he wanted to make a difference in the world. He entered a competition designed to encourage generosity and volunteerism. Ryan took his Christmas money and purchased 100 pairs of socks for the homeless. His parents drove him to the Nashville Union Mission, an hour from their home, and helped him distribute warm socks to homeless men and women.

The boy's idea won the runner-up prize money of $250. With it he bought 500 more pairs of socks for the homeless. His generosity serves as a lesson to all of us. Evidently Ryan understands some basic principles regarding money.

When we come to God, He changes our body language. Taking our tightly clenched fists, He makes them into open hands that offer what we have to benefit His kingdom. In the Korean culture people give their gifts with both hands. They do this to communicate: "I'm not holding anything back. I'm giving you all that I have to offer." Practice this attitude with God, and see how it serves to draw you closer to the One for whom you hunger.

Ray Boltz is a Christian singer/songwriter who has composed a powerful song about giving entitled "What if I Give All?" During each of his concerts, Ray invites people to sponsor a child through a ministry called Mission of Mercy, a Christian organization devoted to feeding hungry people throughout the world.

Several years ago a 3-year-old boy saw the images of hungry children displayed on the large video screen as Boltz sang. When the boy pointed to the screen and asked his mother why that particular child was hungry, she explained how his parents didn't have enough money to buy food. Her son then reached into his pocket and pulled out a $1 bill. "How many will this feed?" he asked. His mother told him it would provide about 10 meals. The little boy immediately asked, "What if I give all I have?"

After learning about the child's generous perspective, Boltz cowrote "What if I Give All?" with his road manager and guitarist, Mark Pay.

Martin Luther would have agreed with Mr. Boltz's song. He wrote: "I have tried to keep things in my hands and lost them all, but what I have given into God's hands I still possess."

Place your trust in God, not in your money. Joyfully use your means to meet the needs of the gospel and the poor. As you do, I believe you will feel your own hunger pangs easing, for through trusting God, you will begin to satisfy your hunger for Him.

EXERCISES:

* ❖ Pray that God will teach you to value that which is of greatest value. Pray that He will change your attitudes about money and make you a generous person. Ask God to give you a heart of genuine concern for those in need.
* ❖ If you are not currently paying tithe, covenant with God to begin. Some people find setting a starting date to be helpful. As they approach the date, they place their financial house in order to enable them to begin returning a faithful tithe to God. Others have begun with a smaller percentage and steadily increased it until they were returning a full 10 percent. Perhaps God is calling you to take a bold leap of faith and begin to return a full tithe today. He calls each of us to trust Him as we become generous people. Prayerfully consider your decision.
* ❖ Once you have begun to return tithe, plan to increase the amount you give to your church and other charities or directly to people in need. Ask God to show you how to be a cheerful giver and to help you develop the trait of generosity.
* ❖ Make a detailed plan to eliminate all debt in your life. Learn to limit "wants" while concentrating on "needs." Free up as much cash for debt reduction as possible. Cut up credit cards in order to avoid the temptation of sliding back into debt. Learn to live on a "cash only" basis. This will free up more funds for charitable giving. It also helps you place a proper value on material things, while enabling you to live free from any creditor's grip.

CHAPTER 10

Trust

(Psalm 57)

What sees you through difficult times in your life?
The people of Gee's Bend, Alabama, have found strength for difficult times in their religious faith. Gee's Bend is a remote, historically Black community occupying a bulb of bottom land, a U-shaped peninsula five miles across and seven miles long, hemmed in on three sides by the Alabama River. Approximately 750 people, comprising about 100 families, live in Gee's Bend today. Almost all of the residents of Gee's Bend are descendants of slaves who worked the plantation that once stood on that site. Joseph Gee laid claim to the land in the early 1800s. He sold the land to his relative, Mark Pettway, in 1845, but the area retained his name.

After the Civil War the freed slaves took the name Pettway and became tenant farmers for the Pettway family. They lived in such desperate poverty that they could scarcely tell the difference between slavery and working as sharecroppers. Every year they went into debt to purchase cottonseed. Their harvests barely paid off the loans, leaving little to live on. This continued until the price of cotton fell by 50 percent. The residents of Gee's Bend were unable to pay their debts. As a result, their creditors seized all of their farming equipment, including shovels and hoes, leaving them with no way to farm and feed themselves. During this time they lived on wild berries, fish from the river, and squirrels they managed to kill with slingshots.

Because of geography and poverty, they were nearly isolated from the surrounding world. At the time the first human being was walking on the moon, the residents of Gee's Bend were 15 miles from the nearest telephone and 50 miles from the nearest supermarket. They crossed the river by ferry, and then walked into the town of Camden, to conduct what little business they could afford to do.

In 1965 the residents of the small community made one of their rare trips away from their homes in order to join Dr. Martin Luther King, Jr., in his march on Selma, Alabama. The "Benders," as people referred to the group, had been so isolated for so long that they were very different from the others who joined the procession. In fact, the other civil rights marchers referred to the Benders as "the Africans," because of how different they seemed. The Benders, along with the other marchers, suffered beatings and arrest for their participation in the march. When the Benders returned home, they used the ferry to make their way into Camden, Alabama, to register to vote.

About that time, the White sheriff of Camden, with the help of a small group of men, burned the ferryboat in order to keep the Benders from crossing the river to register to vote. He said, "We didn't burn the ferry because they are Negroes. We burned the ferry because they forgot they were Negroes." What sustained this community through all the decades of poverty, privation, and prejudice? They will tell you it was their deep faith in Christ.

During the Depression the women of Gee's Bend began making quilts out of old clothes, towels, rags, and virtually any other material they could find, to wrap around their children during cold nights. The families lived in wooden shanties, insulated only by old newspapers the women attached to the inner walls of their homes. So the quilts were useful for keeping their families warm. The quilts bore geometric designs. The women handed down the skills of quilting from one generation to the next.

The women had no idea that the quilts would ever have any value beyond their practical application. But Bill Arnett, an art historian, saw the quilts and visited the women to discuss their artistic relevance. Today the quilts have become some of the most honored and prized artwork of the twentieth century, garnering praise from art historians and collectors worldwide.

The women of Gee's Bend are known for their artwork, and they will tell you that the beautiful quilts they make depict their spiritual beliefs. Their spirituality is equally represented in their music. To this day, the gospel choir of Gee's Bend performs songs with a fervor that is an unmistakable mark of a deep, abiding faith. In 1941 Robert Sonkin recorded a number of gospel songs sung by the residents, both men and women. Their beliefs are still very strong today.

An abiding faith in God has seen the residents of Gee's Bend from the horror of slavery, through the poverty of sharecropping, through the oppression and prejudice of the civil rights movement, to international fame as folk artists.

What is it that sees you through difficult times?

David learned that God was available to help in every situation. Early in his life, he had been a fugitive from King Saul. Fleeing from the king, he hid in a cave near Adullam. At first he lived alone. Eventually David's brothers and 400 distressed, indebted, disgruntled, and discontented men joined him in that cave. Most likely he wrote the psalm during the early part of his sojourn there, while he was still alone. Let's begin with the first five verses.

Psalm 57:1-5

"Have mercy on me, O God, have mercy on me, for in you my soul takes refuge. I will take refuge in the shadow of your wings until the disaster has passed. I cry out to God Most High, to God, who fulfills [his purpose] for me. He sends from heaven and saves me, rebuking those who hotly pursue me; God sends his love and his faithfulness. I am in the midst of lions; I lie among ravenous beasts—men whose teeth are spears and arrows, whose tongues are sharp swords. Be exalted, O God, above the heavens; let your glory be over all the earth."

We can divide the psalm into two sections. The first is a confident cry for deliverance; the second is a commitment to praise God for deliverance. The first section begins with David pleading for mercy even as he takes refuge in God.

Verse 1

"Have mercy on me, O God, have mercy on me, for in you my soul takes refuge. I will take refuge in the shadow of your wings until the disaster has passed."

Notice that David does not call his refuge the cave, but rather God. David may have been hiding in the dank, dark recesses of the cave of Adullam, but it was under the wings of the Almighty that he found safety.

We all live in danger of thinking that we will find our security in anything other than God. Trusting in national defense, in our savings, in our friends, or in our own talents is always a mistake. Placing our trust in anything other than God is a prescription for disaster.

TRUST

David puts his trust in God. We can see this demonstrated in the number of references He makes to the Lord, either by name or by pronoun. He refers to Him nearly 20 times. In addition, he also alludes to God by other words and phrases, such as "refuge" and "shadow of your wings." It reminds us that the focus must always be on God. When we are in trouble, it is easy to look at the difficulty rather than at God. Looking at the problem accomplishes only one thing—making it seem larger and larger, until we become convinced that there exists absolutely no way around it. We feel trapped, helpless, hopeless, and, eventually, depressed.

Looking at God helps us see that He is bigger than our problem, that He is stronger than our enemies. If we focus on Him, our problems seem smaller and smaller, until we realize just how insignificant they really are. The phrase "in the shadow of your wings" is a particularly rich one. At least two images come to mind when examining it.

First, the most frequent Old Testament use of the word "wings" is to refer to the wings of the cherubim on the lid of the ark of the covenant. You will remember that the ark of the covenant was the only article of furniture in the Jewish Temple's Most Holy Place—a chamber so holy that it was entered only once a year on the Day of Atonement, and then only by the high priest. The ark symbolized the throne of God Himself. A rectangular box overlaid with gold, it had on top the mercy seat, a gold representation of a pillow upon which God symbolically sat. Under the mercy seat, inside the ark, rested the tablets of stone containing the written Ten Commandments, God's holy law. This law is an expression of His character.

On top of the ark, one on either side of the mercy seat, stood two golden cherubim with wings outstretched over the mercy seat. It was between the wings and over the mercy seat that God's presence, His Shekinah glory, was to abide. Therefore, to be "in the shadow of your wings" is to be on the mercy seat and under the Shekinah. David is saying that he is as secure as though he were in the Most Holy Place, virtually sitting in God's lap.

We can, however, look at the phrase "in the shadow of your wings" in a second way. Others see it as referring to David being under God's wings. Some protest that God does not have wings. While I am inclined to agree, He has used wings as a metaphor describing His care for those He loves.

In Exodus God said to the children of Israel, "You yourselves have seen what I did to Egypt, and how I carried you on eagles' wings and brought you to myself" (Ex. 19:4). Deuteronomy 32 compares Him to "an eagle that stirs up its nest and hovers over its young, that spreads its wings to catch them and carries them on its pinions" (Deut. 32:11).

This same phrase, "shadow of your wings," occurs in three other psalms. If we were to take the metaphor literally, it would suggest that David is in such close proximity to God that God's shadow—the shadow of His wings—falls upon David in such a way that he can hide from his enemies. It is a picture of perfect protection and of absolute safety.

David is able to rest securely in the Lord's protection since, as he phrases it, He is the "God Most High." That means that there is none greater, none stronger, and none more faithful to His promises than God. Even though he feels as if he is "in the midst of lions" and other "ravenous beasts," during difficult times David can find his security in his God. So, too, we can seek protection and safety in this same deity. Like David, we must cry out to God. He will not let us down.

Perhaps you've heard the story of the tourist to the Grand Canyon who came too close to the edge, lost his footing, and plunged over the side. Just before he fell into space, he happened to grab a rather small bush with both hands. He hung there, his life in the balance, his body tenuously suspended over the great chasm below.

"Is there anyone up there?" he shouted at the sky.

With a rumbling of thunder a mighty voice answered from the sky, "Yes, there is."

"Can you help me?"

The calm voice replied, "Yes, I can. Do you believe?" it continued.

"Yes, yes, I believe."

"Do you have faith?"

"Yes, yes. I have strong faith."

"Well, in that case, simply let loose of the bush, and everything will turn out fine."

After a tense pause the tourist yelled, "Is there anyone else up there?"

Letting go of our hold on the bush is the most difficult thing in the world for us to do. How can you trust God when disaster appears to be certain? David finds himself in this predicament. King Saul wants to kill him, so he hides in a cave. While there, David seeks God for deliverance. But he also decides that even though it seems to defy logic, he is going to trust Him at all costs.

John Powell writes: "Most of us, in our desire for meaningful faith, seem to be saying to God: 'Show me, and I'll believe!' This approach never works. God has made it very clear to us, in the life and teaching of His Son

Jesus, that the process must be reversed. He is saying to us: 'Believe in Me, and I'll show you.'"

How does David commit to such radical belief? As he cries to God for help, he focuses on Him rather than on the problem, and that alone seems to help David. When he makes this conscious decision to trust the Lord, everything changes for him. God's response to his cry for help amazes the fugitive.

Verse 6

"They spread a net for my feet—I was bowed down in distress. They dug a pit in my path—but they have fallen into it themselves."

David sees the plans that his enemies have carefully set for him, and his initial response was one of distress. Who wouldn't react that way? But when David relinquishes his problem to God, the Lord allows his enemies to fall into their own trap. As a result of that single experience, he rejoices.

Verses 7-11

"My heart is steadfast, O God, my heart is steadfast; I will sing and make music. Awake, my soul! Awake, harp and lyre! I will awaken the dawn. I will praise you, O Lord, among the nations; I will sing of you among the peoples. For great is your love, reaching to the heavens; your faithfulness reaches to the skies. Be exalted, O God, above the heavens; let your glory be over all the earth."

When David takes the bold step of trusting God, the Lord is faithful to him. And when God is faithful, David's response is that he will be faithful in turn, and will sing praises to Him. Although David's enemies set a trap for him, he responds with a radical trust in God. God allows David's enemies to ensnare themselves. When David sees that, his heart jumps for joy. Verse 7 describes the emotions he feels as he witnesses God's faithfulness to him.

Verse 7

"My heart is steadfast, O God, my heart is steadfast; I will sing and make music."

What does David sing? He utters a song of praise and exaltation to God. His voice fills the earth with praise to the Deity who has delivered him.

111

Verses 9–11

"**I will praise you, O Lord, among the nations; I will sing of you among the peoples. For great is your love, reaching to the heavens; your faithfulness reaches to the skies. Be exalted, O God, above the heavens; let your glory be over all the earth.**"

David finds relief from his difficulties when he focuses his attention on God's ability to deliver. And when he does that, the Lord rescues him. His response to divine deliverance is to focus his attention even more keenly on God through a song of praise and adoration. As a result David discovers something that we all need to learn: we were created to praise God, and until we do, we will never be whole.

We do not trust God, in part, because we do not praise Him. Nor do we believe that He really is as good as the Bible says He is. And so, like the tourist hanging on to the scraggly plant just over the ledge of the Grand Canyon, we wait, hoping for a better deal to come along. But there is no better deal than God's. And the only way to experience what He wants for us is to trust Him enough to let go.

But how do we do that? Letting go and letting God requires a special type of prayer, one that we can call the prayer of relinquishment. Because our will tends to be in conflict with God's will, we struggle against Him, as we beg, pout, and demand. When He doesn't go along with our plans, we become depressed or we panic. Believe it or not, our struggle over this conflict of wills is a part of the process of satisfying our hunger for God. Fighting this battle is an aspect of growing in our faith as we learn to depend on spiritual resources instead of material or human ones.

The prayer of relinquishment helps us move through the struggle to a firm trust in God. Through it we hand over our problems to Him. More important, we relinquish our very lives to God. We give Him permission to do as He wants with our lives, since we believe that He will do only that which is best for us.

The best place to learn this prayer is from Jesus Himself. He spent the night before His crucifixion in prayer. Leading His disciples to a spot known as Gethsemane, He asked them to pray for Him. But the disciples fell asleep, leaving Him to pray alone.

What did Jesus pray? At first He asked to be delivered from the cross. "Let this cup pass" was His prayer (see Matt. 26:39). Sweat mixed with blood oozed from His pores as He wrestled through that clash of wills. What He desired was not what God wanted. And what was the result of His great struggle? "Not My will but Yours be done," He finally prayed (see verse 42).

This is the prayer of relinquishment. It is a decision to ask that God's will, rather than our own, be done in our lives. Jesus wept as He engaged in this great battle. It was a gut-wrenching experience—and it always is.

We crave whatever we want so badly that we can taste it. The last thing we desire is pain or loss. But we must believe that God knows best, trusting that the One who created us, and who redeemed us, will not take us through anything that would not be for our best good.

As we trust His will and relinquish our own will to Him, we find a sweetness we never knew possible before. Suddenly we feel our stomachs being filled with the very best of food—the food we have hungered for all our lives. It is the food of God—God Himself being ingested into our very beings and satisfying us as nothing else ever has, or ever could. It is the feeling that comes when we bravely let go of the silly, shallow things we so desperately have clung to, and find that God really is trustworthy.

A. W. Tozer wrote that "what we need very badly these days is a company of Christians who are prepared to trust God as completely now as they must do at the last day. For each of us the time is surely coming when we shall have nothing but God! Health and wealth and friends and hiding places will all be swept away, and we shall have only God. To the man of pseudo faith that is a terrifying thought, but to real faith it is one of the most comforting thoughts the heart can entertain."

Now, we must recognize that this does not mean that when we trust God, nothing bad will ever afflict us. What happened to Jesus when He prayed His prayer of relinquishment? He was strengthened, to be sure, but He was also crucified. Jesus trusted and died. But He knew that it was better to relinquish the will and physically die than it was to hold on and perish from another kind of death—spiritual death. It is always best to be in the will of God.

What I'm saying may not make sense to some of you. But God's way of doing things does not always seem reasonable to the human mind. His way does not always fit human logic. But it is always the best way.

James Eads built the first steel bridge in America. It spanned the Mississippi River at St. Louis. The bridge had its detractors. Many had argued that it could not be built. They claimed that steel was too heavy, and that the bridge would collapse, unable to support its own weight. But Eads built the bridge anyway, and it did not collapse. Now many protested that the bridge was a disaster waiting to happen. They said that, while it was obviously standing, it would never support the weight of a train laden with passengers and cargo.

In answer to these critics, Eads ordered 14 locomotives to stop on the bridge at once. He had them sit there all day long. When people saw that nothing happened, they decided that the bridge was trustworthy and began to label it the eighth wonder of the world.

God is summoning us to a leap of faith. He calls us to deny what our eyes see and what our gut tells us, and to trust solely in Him. As Stormie Omartian has written: "Trust that God has your best interests in mind and be willing to do what he asks of you, even if you don't understand why. Obedience starts with having a heart that says yes to God."

In the summer of 1988 Ben Patterson and three friends climbed the highest peak in Yosemite National Park. While two of Ben's friends were experienced mountaineers, he was not. As the climb progressed, the two experienced mountaineers opened up a wide gap between Ben and his less-experienced companion.

Being competitive by nature, Ben began to look for shortcuts he might be able to take to beat them to the top. Thinking that he saw one to the right of an outcropping of rock, he went up it despite warnings from the more experienced climbers that his choice was not a good choice. Soon he found himself trapped in a cul-de-sac. Below him was several hundred feet of a sheer slope of ice, pitched at a 45-degree angle. Ben was only 10 feet from the safety of a rock, but one mistake would send him plummeting to the valley floor and certain death.

The more experienced climbers told him to wait while they positioned themselves to help him. While standing on the rock Ben had wanted to reach, one of his friends used an ice axe to carve two footsteps into the glacier. Then he said, "Ben, you must step out from where you are and put your foot where the first foothold is. . . . Without a moment's hesitation swing your other foot across and land it on the next step. . . . [Then] reach out and I will take your hand and pull you to safety. But listen carefully: As you step across, don't lean into the mountain! If anything, lean out a bit. Otherwise, your feet could fly out from under you, and you will start sliding down."

Ben admits that when he stands on the edge of a cliff, it is his habit to press as close to the mountain as possible—to become one with it. He certainly does not want to lean away from it. But Ben trusted his friend, and decided against going by what he felt and instead put his confidence in the more experienced climber. Leaning out, he stepped to the safety of the other man's arm.

God calls us to act against our instincts and trust Him—not because it will make our life easier or even protect us from harm, but solely because it will satisfy our longing for Him. Trust Him today. We must trust God with our past, our present, and most certainly our future. He is worthy of our trust.

EXERCISES:

Trusting God requires that we realize that He is God and that we are not. This is what philosopher Peter Kreeft calls the "grammar of existence." In order to trust God, we must first acknowledge that He is in charge by humbling ourselves to accept His will and not our own. We must endeavor to be obedient to all His commands. Perhaps it is not a bad idea to begin and end all of our requests with the prayer of Mary: "I am the Lord's servant,' Mary answered. 'May it be to me as you have said'" (Luke 1:38).

❖ Pray Psalm 57 every day for a week. Ask God to help you trust Him completely, even when you are oppressed.

❖ Are you currently experiencing a conflict with God over something you want to do that you believe may not be in accordance with His will? Bravely submit the matter to God through the prayer of relinquishment. Surrender the matter entirely to Him and refuse to act until you see clear evidence that your next move is God's will for your life.

❖ Write the following texts on 3" x 5" cards. Place them where you will encounter them during the day, i.e., in your purse or wallet, on the corner of your bedroom or bathroom mirror, taped to the dashboard of your car, on your computer monitor, etc. Read each card at least three times each time you find it, and pray the text, claiming it as a promise. Learn to pray these texts with every decision of life, whether large or small: Psalm 9:10; 13:5; Psalm 25:2; 31:14; 32:10; 37:5; 52:8; 56:3, 4, 11; 62:8; 91:2; 115:11; 118:8; 125:1; 143:8; 146:3; Proverbs 3:5; Isaiah 26:3, 4; 2 Corinthians 1:9; Hebrews 2:13.

CHAPTER 11

Rest

(Psalm 92)

When my children were small, they liked the stories of Winnie the Pooh. Pooh is the bear that belongs to Christopher Robin. Toward the end of one Winnie-the-Pooh story, Christopher Robin told Pooh that he would soon be going to school. It meant that he would be "going away."

"Now there comes a time in everyone's life when toys and games are replaced by pencils and books. You see, Christopher Robin was going away to school. Nobody in the forest knew exactly why or where he was going, all they knew was that it had something to do with twice times and ABCs and where a place called Brazil is.

"'Pooh, what do you like doing best in the world?'

"'What I like best is me going to visit you and saying, "How about a smackerel of honey?"'

"'I like that too, but what I like doing best is Nothing.'

"'How do you do Nothing?'

"'Well, it's when grown-ups ask, "What are you going to do?" and you say "Nothing." And you go and do it.'

"'I like that, let's do it all the time.'

"'You know something, Pooh, I'm not going to do just Nothing anymore.'

"'You mean never again?'

"'Well, not so much.'"

Is there ever a time when you "do nothing"? When you just simply rest? Everyone needs rest—and not just the kind that we get at night when we lie down for five, six, or, if we're very fortunate, seven hours or more,

116

although that type of rest is very important.

When I was in high school, I was fortunate enough to have a part in the school play. That year we presented *Our Town,* by Thornton Wilder. I played the part of the stage manager, a man who gives commentary on the characters and goings-on in Grover's Corners, New Hampshire, where the play is set. But the stage manager also shares insights on life. Toward the conclusion of the play he speaks of the endless cycle of life and death, and of the stress and strain that life places on each of us. The living carry heavy burdens—so heavy, in fact, that "the strain's so bad that every 16 hours everybody lies down and gets a rest."

Without daily rest, life's burdens are too heavy for any of us to bear. Nightly slumber renews us, and helps us face the vicissitudes of another day. God knew how fragile our lives would be, so He designed the universe in such a way that every day begins in darkness, for the purpose of dormancy. We commence each day with rest.

As welcome as this is, it is still not enough for our frail frames. If we are to survive our hectic existence, we need something more than just a good night's sleep. God knew that we would require a more significant, a weekly, time of rest. We must have time to step outside the demands of efficiency and productivity. He also recognized that we would need permission to do absolutely nothing—to rest and renew ourselves both in body and soul.

I made a presentation about rest to a group of young couples, and after the meeting a young mother of two small children said, "You mean it's OK with God if I rest?" Not only is it OK with Him but He actually commands it.

God, from the creation of the world, instituted a weekly 24-hour period of rest, worship, and renewal. He called such time Sabbath. Sabbath is a day of rest and worship. It is an appointment with, and invitation to, fellowship with the One who alone can give us rest. Sabbath is an opportunity to put everything else on hold—all outside appointments, all of the hustle and bustle of everyday living—and focus on activities that restore and renew our bodies and souls. The Sabbath is a time to clear away distractions so that we can discover God's grace in our lives.

The Jews have celebrated the experience of Sabbath throughout their history. Psalm 92 is the only psalm dedicated to the experience of Sabbath rest, and it teaches how we can satisfy our hunger for God through the spiritual practice of rest.

Psalm 92:1-4

"A psalm. A song. For the Sabbath day. It is good to praise the Lord and make music to your name, O Most High, to proclaim your love in the morning and your faithfulness at night, to the music of the ten-stringed lyre and the melody of the harp. For you make me glad by your deeds, O Lord; I sing for joy at the works of your hands."

The psalmist tells us something vital about how to rest. Genuine rest comes not just from a lack of activity, but from actively praising God. Inactivity, something the ancients have called "holy leisure," has its role and value, but the primary purpose of Sabbath rest is praise to God. We are to praise Him all day long through singing, proclamation, and instrumental music.

How is that restful? Praise takes our focus off ourselves and places it on God. In the process we forget our problems and struggles. Often our stress results from focusing on ourselves and our difficulties. Praise takes us away from those issues and helps us concentrate on God's attributes with hearts full of thanksgiving and adoration. In doing that, we come to realize that there exists Someone who is bigger than our problems. Gaining perspective on life, we begin to see ourselves for who we are and our God for who He is. We recognize Him as the one in whom we can find rest. In verse 1 the psalmist says, "It is good to praise the Lord . . ." That reminds me of the language of Creation week.

In the first chapter of Genesis, at the end of each day, God would look at everything He had made and declare it to be "good." Since Psalm 92 speaks of God's creative acts as a reason to praise Him, perhaps the psalmist had Genesis 1 in mind when he wrote. In any case, it is good to praise the Lord—good for our hearts and minds, and good for our perspective on life and the world. Not only does it help our emotional and mental states to praise the Lord, but it is also God's right that we should praise Him. We find our rest in doing this good thing, since to praise God is to fulfill the purpose for which we were made.

Centuries ago the church thought it important to write down the most basic of Christian truths in the form of a confession. Such confessions were simply statements of doctrine. They outlined the basic elements of the faith. One such doctrinal statement is called *The Westminster Shorter Catechism*. In it we find the following question and answer: "What is the chief end of man? Man's chief end is to glorify God and to enjoy Him forever." Every Christian can ascribe to it, because our "chief end," or our ultimate purpose, is to glorify God and enjoy Him. By the way, the two things go together. When we glorify God, we truly enjoy Him, and when we enjoy God, it makes us want to glorify Him.

Sabbath is a day devoted entirely to such activity. It is a day to glorify and enjoy God, and in so doing, we find rest. What do we glorify Him for?

Verse 2
". . . to proclaim your love in the morning and your faithfulness at night."

We are to glorify God for His love and His faithfulness. The word here translated "love" is the Hebrew *hesed*. We referred to the word in earlier chapters. *Hesed* describes God's intense, faithful, and redeeming love for us. As Christians we are to glorify Him for a love so strong that it sent Jesus to the cross in order that He might save us. God's faithfulness is His determination to keep us in the saving relationship given to us through His devoted love. These are words based on relationship. In short, we are to glorify God for His desire for relationship with us, and His willingness to make that relationship happen. Relationship is the key thing here, because it is one that saves.

Sabbath is not a time for legalistic rules and regulations. Nor is it about a list of things that we can and cannot do during that 24-hour period. Rather it is a day about relationships, primarily God's relationship with us, and then our relationship with Him. As a consequence, Sabbath is a time for nurturing relationships.

Gayle and I have a wonderful marriage. It just seems to grow sweeter every day. But such a relationship doesn't just happen. It is not an accident, but something that we must constantly work at. One of the things we do in order to have a strong relationship is that every week Gayle and I have a date night. Even after many years of marriage we have decided that we are going to continue to make time for each other—time simply to enjoy each another. We guard this time from anything extraneous to our relationship. Because we work together as pastors, the church tends to dominate all our conversations. But our rule for our date night is no church talk. Not as a legalistic requirement, but as something we have agreed upon in order to protect and enhance our time together. This way, our date night becomes an opportunity to clear away all the distractions so that we might rediscover the grace that results from our love for each other.

God also thinks that setting a weekly date is a good idea. In fact, that is what the Sabbath is all about. It is a weekly date with God. And just as

Gayle and I have set a few boundaries in order to protect our time together, it is also helpful to establish some boundaries to guard our date with God.

After my date with Gayle I feel loved, refreshed, and more secure in my relationship with her. During our hours together we shut out all distractions and focus on each other.

And similarly during my date with God I shut out all distractions—I turn the television off, I cease from all work, I refuse to putter around the house, I try not to do anything that might distract me from the goal of giving Him glory, and I focus on Him. I don't do these things because of legalistic rules, but that I might protect the time for communion with God. After my date with God I feel loved, refreshed, rested, and more secure in my relationship with Him. It is amazing how refreshing this can be. There is, however, an alternative to this.

Verses 5–9
"How great are your works, O Lord, how profound your thoughts! The senseless man does not know, fools do not understand, that though the wicked spring up like grass and all evildoers flourish, they will be forever destroyed. But you, O Lord, are exalted forever. For surely your enemies, O Lord, surely your enemies will perish; all evildoers will be scattered."

What is the alternative to keeping a regular date with God—to experiencing a day of rest and renewal? That we live like senseless fools. The phrase translated in verse 6 as "the senseless man" could be better rendered as "the brute man." Here the psalmist has in mind people who live like brute beasts, who demonstrate no more understanding than an animal. The biblical writer declares that those who refuse a Sabbath rest behave like brute beasts. They don't take care of relationships that transform, renew, rejuvenate, and save. How much better to find your rest in the God who saves!

During the nineteenth century a group of people wanted to go to California. So they set out from St. Louis, Missouri, traveling together in a wagon train for safety. Soon after they left St. Louis, a disagreement arose among them. One faction desired to get to California as fast as possible, so they wanted to travel seven days a week. The other group preferred to journey for six days, then take a Sabbath day's rest to worship God. The disagreement became so sharp that the wagon train eventually split into two groups, with the first pushing hard seven days a week, and the second group resting one day out of seven.

Guess which group got to California first? The one that traveled only six days a week. The other group's failure to allow time for rest and renewal caused it to go slower because of worn-out animals and people. Those who took the time to renew themselves with a day of rest were able to accomplish more in six days than the others could do in seven.

God's plan to provide for a day of rest for His children demonstrates true genius. As wonderful as this is, however, higher productivity is not the primary reason for celebrating the Sabbath. The purpose of the Sabbath is to find our rest in God—to discover the joys of a deeper fulfillment through a more meaningful relationship in the Deity who saves us.

What are some of the other benefits of celebrating a Sabbath rest?

Verses 10-15

"You have exalted my horn like that of a wild ox; fine oils have been poured upon me. My eyes have seen the defeat of my adversaries; my ears have heard the rout of my wicked foes. The righteous will flourish like a palm tree, they will grow like a cedar of Lebanon; planted in the house of the Lord, they will flourish in the courts of our God. They will still bear fruit in old age, they will stay fresh and green, proclaiming, 'The Lord is upright; he is my Rock, and there is no wickedness in him.'"

People living in an agrarian society composed the psalms. They made their living by raising livestock, growing crops, and hunting wild game. Admiring nature and wild animals, they rejoiced in the fertility of the land. Since these were the things they knew and valued, it was only natural that they drew much of their poetic language—their praise language—from the natural world.

The psalmist tells us that his experience of a deepening, growing relationship with God, as fostered by a weekly Sabbath, has resulted in his feeling the exaltation that a young wild ox must experience when, in the full measure of its strength, it discovers that it is a formidable foe because of the weapon it wears on its head. That horn makes it feel invincible. Its strength and vigor are the joys of its life. Sabbath rest renews our strength and reminds us that God is our protection, much as the wild ox is protected by its horns.

Verse 10 continues with "fine oils have been poured upon me." In that arid land oil of any kind was a precious commodity. It refreshed parched skin and soothed wounds, promoting healing. Oil, in Scripture, symbolizes several things. As we have seen already, it depicts the refreshing of the Holy

Spirit in our lives and represents healing and plenty. The ancients used oil mixed with special spices to anoint a king or a high priest upon assuming office. As the oil ran down on the head and shoulders, it represented the Spirit's outpouring of blessings. So the Sabbath renews our strength, refreshes us, blesses us, and sets us apart as God's special, holy people.

Now contrast these blessings of God's Sabbathkeeping people with the fate of the wicked.

Verse 11

"My eyes have seen the defeat of my adversaries; my ears have heard the rout of my wicked foes."

God's people are blessed by a deepening relationship with Him, while those who do not experience such a relationship ultimately suffer from the poverty of a spirit separated from God.

Now the psalmist returns to the blessings that God's people receive.

Verses 12, 13

"The righteous will flourish like a palm tree, they will grow like a cedar of Lebanon; planted in the house of the Lord, they will flourish in the courts of our God."

While the wicked grow weaker, those who find their rest in God become stronger. But this passage is not speaking so much of physical strength as it is of spiritual. The apostle Paul wrote that "though outwardly we are wasting away, yet inwardly we are being renewed day by day" (2 Cor. 4:16). We find something very special about the spiritual vitality of those who have spent many years resting in relationship with God. They have an energy that cannot be duplicated by any other means.

My father-in-law, Jack Whitacre, was such a person. He always felt close to God, and had a vigorous prayer life. When he was 90 years old, Jack left the church family he had worshipped with for more than 40 years to help plant a new congregation. It had a more contemporary worship style than most people in their 80s or 90s usually enjoy. But he did it because he felt God leading him to do something new and exciting for Him.

Jack left the comfort and security of the familiar to follow God's leading to an uncertain future. He did it at an age when most people would say, "I've done my part. Now it's time for the younger people to do the work." But he was able to do this bold thing for God because he had spent many years flourishing as a palm tree or a cedar planted in the very courts of the most high God.

Verses 14 and 15 give further benefits that come from long years of resting in God.

Verses 14, 15
"They will still bear fruit in old age, they will stay fresh and green, proclaiming, 'The Lord is upright; he is my Rock, and there is no wickedness in him.'"

Retirement is not a biblical concept. That doesn't mean that we cannot retire from a job, but it does mean that it is always wrong to retire from serving God. Those who daily, and weekly, have learned to rest in God will never tire of His service, and they will never cease to bear fruit for Him.

After Joshua led the children of Israel into the Promised Land, a group of stubborn people remained entrenched in a mountainous region. Caleb, one of the original 12 spies from 40 years earlier, was now about 90 years old. He went to Joshua and asked for a new challenge. Telling the Hebrew leader that his eye had not dimmed or his strength diminished, Caleb was eager for something new and challenging to do for God.

So Joshua told him to root out this pocket of Israel's enemies. He promised to give Caleb that land as his inheritance upon completion of the task. Long ago Caleb had learned to rest in God. He found his strength in that relationship. So in his "golden years" he still bore fruit. Caleb was as fresh and green as a new plant in the spring. Such a plant is supple and vigorous. So too are those who have learned to find their rest in God.

Sabbath shows us how to do such great things. It teaches us to rest in God as we are renewed by His strength. Those who do so throughout the course of life will have a testimony for God that remains strong to the very end. We find many examples in the Bible. Moses lived to be 120 years old. Even in his old age, he praised God. He finished the last book of the Pentateuch, Deuteronomy, with some of his best writing.

Jacob spoke his most encouraging words at the end of his life. The same is true of Joseph, who praised God all the way to the end of his earthly existence. Although he had long ago forgiven his brothers for what they had done to him, he again reminded them of his forgiveness at the end of his life. He also spoke of God's sovereignty in using that which the brothers intended for evil, in order to accomplish His great purposes.

Paul did some of his best work late in life, and as he faced death he was able to proclaim that he had fought the fight, had run the race, and had finished the course. His gaze was not toward the past, but forward, in anticipation of that which God had in store for him in heaven.

John wrote the book of Revelation while living on the island of Patmos, when he was a very old man. His gaze was set forward as he concluded his book with "Even so, come, Lord Jesus" (Rev. 22:20, KJV).

Sabbath makes relationship a priority. Those who observe it discover a deeper relationship with God that renews and refreshes. The rest provided in that relationship adds years to life, and positive energy to those years. Our world is so fast paced that we forget that relationships take time to grow, whether they be with God, friends, or family. The Sabbath gives us time to grow relationships, allowing leisurely conversations, whether they be with fellow human beings or with God. Thus Sabbath time is absolutely necessary if we are to satisfy our hunger for God.

"To fail to see the value of simply being with God and 'doing nothing,'" Leonard Doohan writes, "is to miss the heart of Christianity. . . . If in life we are not still, cannot be inspired by the beauty around us, cannot concentrate or be silent, how then can we suddenly achieve this in prayer?"

Prayer and meditation cannot develop without patterns of quiet and leisure. Sabbath teaches us to experience "holy leisure," and to build times to do nothing into our schedules. It enables us to develop a friendship with God.

A wise old pastor was once lying down, relaxing underneath the warm sun, when a hunter came rushing toward him. Seeing the pastor, the hunter stopped and then chastised him for taking it so easy. "Surely a man of God should be busy about his work."

Sitting up, the minister looked at the hunter and said, "Take your bow and shoot an arrow." The hunter, not wanting to offend the pastor further, reluctantly obliged. Then the pastor repeated the instruction again, and again, and again. It continued until the hunter finally said, "But sir, if I keep my bow stretched all the time, it will break."

"Precisely," the wise pastor replied. "And so it is with us human beings. We too will break if we push ourselves without taking time out to relax."

God commands us to take time to relax. In order to facilitate that, He created the Sabbath. Sabbath is a day of rest and fellowship. It is a time to grow a friendship with God through worship, praise, adoration, and yes, even through "holy leisure." Determine that today will be the day you begin to experience God's Sabbath rest.

EXERCISES:

❖ In obedience to God, set aside a 24-hour Sabbath time each week. Remember that when God established the Sabbath, it began on Friday evening with the setting of the sun and ended Saturday evening as the sun set on that day. Determine that you will not work on the Sabbath day, but that you will devote the entire time to rest. That does not mean that you will sleep its hours away. But it does mean that you will not work on that day. Select which activities you need to avoid in order to protect the time. Spend the day in worship, meditation, prayer, Bible study, and fellowship with family and fellow believers. Use some of the time to bless others, perhaps those who are in need.

❖ To make this time special, choose to welcome the beginning of your Sabbath with the lighting of candles, a prayer welcoming the Sabbath, a simple meal, and with scripture and song. It may be helpful to read or pray Psalm 92 as you begin the Sabbath. Choose to end the Sabbath in much the same way, with scripture, prayer, or perhaps even a meal. Have the beginning and ending of the Sabbath be of extra significance so as to make the time stand out as special.

❖ In addition to a Sabbath day, find additional "Sabbath moments" during your week. They will be periods of "holy leisure," times of resting in God through worship, praise, and prayer.

❖ Pray that God will teach you to rest in Him in all things. Pray that the rest He gives will not only be on the Sabbath day, but that it will be a part of your daily life.

CHAPTER 12

Praise

(Psalm 146)

Tim Kimmel tells of concert pianist Andor Foldes who, when he was 72, recalled a turning point in his career. When Foldes was 16, he was already a skilled pianist, living in Budapest. But he was at his personal all-time low because of a conflict with his piano teacher. It was a very difficult year for the young man.

During that same year Emil von Sauer came to Budapest for a concert. While there, Sauer learned of Andor Foldes and requested that the young pianist play for him. It was a real honor, for not only was Sauer an extremely gifted pianist, but he was also the last surviving pupil of Franz Liszt.

Foldes performed some of the most difficult works of Bach, Beethoven, and Schumann. When he finished, Sauer walked over to him and kissed him on the forehead. "My son," he said, "when I was your age I became a student of Liszt. He kissed me on the forehead after my first lesson, saying, 'Take good care of this kiss—it comes from Beethoven, who gave it to me after hearing me play. I have waited for years to pass on this sacred heritage, but now I feel you deserve it.'"

Praise is powerful. It is a pity that we hear so little of it today. That fact reminds me of something the Duke of Wellington said regarding praise. You will remember that Napoleon and his French army seemed unstoppable. No one had been able to withstand them. The inhabitants of the British Isles feared that if something did not halt him, his next move would be to invade England. The nation called upon the Duke of Wellington to prevent a Napoleonic invasion of his homeland, and through a set of seemingly miraculous events, he stopped the French emperor at Waterloo.

Wellington became an instant hero in England. But those who served under his command found him difficult to please. While the duke was brilliant, he was also demanding. He was not a man given to compliments for his subordinates. Praise seldom came from his lips. In his old age Wellington regretted his leadership style. As he faced the final chapters of his life, a young woman asked him what, if anything, he would do differently if he could live his life over. The aged duke thought for a moment, and then said, "I'd give more praise."

The Duke of Wellington appears, in his later years, to have discovered that which the psalms have taught for centuries. Praise is to be an essential element in the diet of human beings. Not just praise in general but a more specific form of praise is required for all who would live life well.

Everyone who has experienced hunger for the living God will follow the psalmists' lead and develop the habit of praise. Habitual praise to God helps us satisfy our hunger for Him. As important and as good as it is to praise others, it is of even more vital to praise God.

The last section of the Psalter, Psalms 146-150, all begin and end with the word "hallelujah," translated as "praise the Lord" by most of our English versions. The last five psalms differ from those in the rest of the book in that they do not contain material on the author's grief, shame, sins, doubts, or fears. While the earlier psalms spoke of such things, all of that is missing from the final five psalms. We are left with pure praise and nothing else.

Psalm 146:1-4

"Praise the Lord. Praise the Lord, O my soul. I will praise the Lord all my life; I will sing praise to my God as long as I live. Do not put your trust in princes, in mortal men, who cannot save. When their spirit departs, they return to the ground; on that very day their plans come to nothing."

Pastor Roy Clements has said that three words are understood in almost every language on earth. They are "amen," "hallelujah," and "Coca-Cola."

Commentator James Montgomery Boice tells us that "hallelujah" is a compound word. It consists of two Hebrew words. The first word is *hallel,* which means "praise." The second is *jah,* a contraction of the name for God, Yahweh (or "Jehovah"). Hallelujah means "praise the Lord." It became a regular response in Jewish worship. The worship leader would say something that the congregation agreed with, and the congregation would respond, "Hallelujah."

Now, we should not use the word carelessly or thoughtlessly. It is important that the congregation listen closely for some word of Scripture, or some word from the worship leader or pastor that has the ring of truth, and then it can respond with "Hallelujah."

This means that we need to work at worship. We are to be involved in it and pay careful attention while being ready to respond. Praise is to be given to God because of who He is, and because of what He does. But to do that, we must understand something of His character as revealed in Scripture. Worship is based on the process of thinking about what God is like and what He has done.

Of course, none of this would be possible if He had not revealed Himself in Scripture, the primary way God has disclosed Himself to us. Therefore, true worship is not possible without an understanding of God's Word. The Bible is to be the centerpiece of our praise. Without Scripture, our praise lacks understanding. It sounds insincere and shallow. But when Scripture is the basis of our worship, such worship has depth, value, and real meaning.

Although Scripture is the basis of our praise, it is also important that our praise bear our personal imprint. The psalmist says:

Verse 2
"I will praise the Lord all my life; I will sing praise to my God as long as I live."

What will you praise God for today? What elements of His character mean the most to you just now? What has He done for you that should elicit gratitude to Him from your lips? Praise is to be a lifelong habitual pursuit for those who would satisfy their hunger for God.

C. S. Lewis explains the value of praise when he writes: "I think we delight to praise what we enjoy because the praise not merely expresses but completes the enjoyment. . . . It is not out of compliment that lovers keep on telling one another how beautiful they are; the delight is incomplete till it is expressed."

The more you praise God, the more you appreciate Him and the closer you feel to Him. And the closer you feel to God and the greater your appreciation for all that He has done for you, the more you long to praise Him. This eternal circle becomes our delight.

Praise does, however, have some dangers. The psalmist addresses these in verses 3 and 4.

Verses 3, 4

"Do not put your trust in princes, in mortal men, who cannot save. When their spirit departs, they return to the ground; on that very day their plans come to nothing."

The psalmist warns us about placing a greater value on people than we do on God, something easy to do since we cannot see the Lord. After all, we do see and interact with people every day.

Often God works through people to bless us. But we must always remember that the blessings that come our way originated in Him. People are only the vehicle He uses to bring those blessings to us. At times people may be wonderful vehicles, but they are not dependable. They are weak, undependable, and temporary, while God is strong, absolutely dependable, and eternal. It is better by far to place our trust in God.

In verses 3 and 4 the psalmist employs a play on words that would be easy to miss in the English translation. In Hebrew the word *adam* means both "man" and "earth" or "ground." It is foolish to trust in mortal men since eventually they return to the *adam,* or ground. Dirt will once more become dirt. Verse 4 reminds us of Genesis 3:19: "For dust you are and to dust you will return." The word translated as "dust" is *adam.* The second play on words involves the Hebrew word *ruach,* which means, "spirit" or "breath." The psalmist writes:

Verse 4

"When their spirit departs, they return to the ground; on that very day their plans come to nothing."

Many assume that "spirit" and "soul" are the same thing. The Bible writers did not make such a mistake. *"Ruach"* simply means "breath," and suggests no conscious entity. Verse 4 reminds us that when the last breath leaves our bodies, our thoughts cease, our plans come to an end, and we have no more consciousness until the resurrection of the dead at the Second Coming, which occurs for those who trust in Jesus at the Second Coming.

From this we learn that life is fragile, existing one breath to the next. And when we exhale our last breath, our thoughts, hopes, dreams, fears, and worries all cease until God chooses to give us life again.

God is eternal. The Life-giver, He depends on no one for His existence. It is far better to praise Him than to praise human beings. And it is far better to place our trust in God than in humanity. Turning that thought around, it is far better not to trust in the praise of men, but only in the praise of the eternal God, for only He is wise enough to give good praise.

When Academy Award-winning actor Charlton Heston was a young struggling actor, he worked with Laurence Olivier on Broadway. The play they did was not very good, so the critics hated and destroyed it. "Before the opening-night party," Heston said later, "we were doomed." A short while later he found himself in a restaurant with Olivier. "I suppose you learn how to forget the bad notices," Heston commented.

Olivier gripped his elbow and said, "Laddie! What's much harder, and far more important, is that you have to learn to forget the good ones."

We must not place our trust in the praise or support of temporary dust. Instead, we must put it in God and in His praise. And we must learn to give praise to Him, for He alone is eternal, wise, and absolutely trustworthy. The praise of human beings is a dangerous thing to have confidence in.

In 1066 William the Conqueror defeated King Harold at the Battle of Hastings, a victory that changed the course of history for Great Britain and, to some degree, the entire Western world. William enjoyed the adoration of his subjects for his triumph. He was on top of the world. That is, until the year 1087. William went to war with the French, under King Philip, and was on the verge of celebrating a great victory when his horse stumbled, throwing him forward against the iron pommel of his saddle. Believe it or not, the resulting injury was fatal. Servants carried the king to safety, but he died a short time later.

His nobles, frightened that their ruler's death signaled certain defeat, raced home in an attempt to protect their own possessions from the French. William's servants stripped his body of clothing and jewelry and fled for their lives. The dead body of the great conqueror of England lay naked, abandoned by nobles and servants alike.

The psalmist, in Psalm 146, reminds us that we are never to place our trust in mere mortals, regardless of their fame or power. We are not to trust human praise, but are to trust only in the God of heaven.

Verses 3, 4

"Do not put your trust in princes, in mortal men, who cannot save. When their spirit departs, they return to the ground; on that very day their plans come to nothing."

Scripture constantly emphasizes that God alone is worthy of our praise and out trust. He alone can be depended upon without reservation. What blessings do we receive when we do exactly that?

Verse 5

"Blessed is he whose help is the God of Jacob, whose hope is in the Lord his God."

Those who refuse to put their hope in human beings, but instead place their confidence in God, will receive blessings. The name used here to refer to God suggests the type of blessings they will receive. Nine times the last six verses of the psalm call God, in our English translation, "the Lord." The word translated "the Lord" is the Hebrew "Yahweh" (often rendered "Jehovah"), the covenant name for God. The implication is that those who trust in Him rather than in human beings will be rewarded with a deeper relationship with the covenant-keeping God.

Verse 5

"Blessed is he whose help is the God of Jacob, whose hope is in the Lord his God."

Throughout Scripture, when God makes a promise of reward, He is the reward. The very best gift that He ever gives is that of Himself. He is that for which we hunger, everything we have ever needed, and the only thing we ever will need.

When John Wesley was 21 years old he went to Oxford. Wesley came from a Christian home, and he was a good-looking young man with a good mind. Perhaps because of this, he was a bit full of himself. One day he was talking to a porter. During the conversation he learned that the man only had one coat and was so poor that he didn't even have a bed. Yet it struck Wesley how cheerful the porter seemed to be. The man continually expressed his gratitude to God.

Wesley had a touch of a smart mouth in those days. His immaturity caused him to make a silly joke about the man's poverty. "And what else do you thank God for?" he quipped sarcastically, and the porter did not miss that fact.

With a smile the porter answered immediately, "I thank Him that He has given me my life and being, a heart to love Him, and above all a constant desire to serve Him!" The man's reply startled Wesley. The porter's sincerity moved John deeply, and brought him to the realization that he knew nothing of the meaning of true gratitude.

Many years later, in 1791, John Wesley lay on his deathbed at the age of 88. Those who gathered around him realized how well he had learned the lesson of praising God in every circumstance. Despite his extreme weakness, he began singing the hymn "I'll Praise My Maker While I've

Breath." Wesley had learned that Jesus was the only thing he ever really needed, and because he had Jesus, he had plenty for which to give praise to God.

Why should you praise God? Jesus Himself repeatedly declares, "I am the life." That means that apart from a relationship with Him, no one lives. He is the Creator, He is the Sustainer, and He is the Redeemer. It is only through Him that we exist. Our hope for salvation rests in God. It is because of Jesus' sacrifice that our need for forgiveness has been met. And only that sacrifice makes intimacy with the Father possible. A relationship of intimacy with God is the greatest gift ever bestowed upon humanity.

Verse 6 tells us that since our only hope is to be found in Him, it is good to know that the Lord is forever faithful.

Verse 6

"The Maker of heaven and earth, the sea, and everything in them—the Lord, who remains faithful forever."

God does not just stop at saving us. Even after He has done that, He remains faithful forever. He never turns His back on us. Instead He declares, "I will never leave thee, nor forsake thee" (Heb. 13:5). It has been my experience that He always keeps His word.

Verse 7 tells us that He frees us from all manner of bondage and captivity.

Verse 7

"He upholds the cause of the oppressed and gives food to the hungry. The Lord sets prisoners free."

The Lord never forsakes or ignores the oppressed and the hungry. They are the objects of His special concern.

When the psalmist declares that the Lord releases prisoners, he is not just talking about those physically incarcerated. Many have never been behind bars. They are prisoners of poverty, guilt, and self-hatred. Jesus liberates us from loneliness, shame, and self-hatred. He sets us free from physical diseases, relational dysfunction, and personal emptiness. Only Jesus can break the bonds of addiction to substances, sex, and pornography. We have no other hope.

You remember what Jesus announced when called on to preach in His hometown of Nazareth, don't you? He quoted from Isaiah 61:1, 2: "The Spirit of the Sovereign Lord is on me, because the Lord has anointed me to preach good news to the poor. He has sent me to bind up the brokenhearted, to proclaim freedom for the captives and release from darkness for the prisoners, to proclaim the year of the Lord's favor and the day of vengeance of our God, to comfort all who mourn."

The freedom from prison spoken of here is a spiritual one from spiritual bondage. "The Lord sets prisoners free."

In verse 8 the psalmist agrees with Isaiah's statement that the Messiah would open the eyes of the blind.

Verse 8

"The Lord gives sight to the blind, the Lord lifts up those who are bowed down, the Lord loves the righteous."

Spiritual blindness is the greatest form of blindness. The book of Revelation speaks of the spiritual blindness that the church at Laodicea suffered. It was the blindness that fails to see its own need: "You say, 'I am rich; I have acquired wealth and do not need a thing.' But you do not realize that you are wretched, pitiful, poor, blind and naked" (Rev. 3:17).

But just as Jesus promises to heal the blindness of Laodicea, so too does He vow to remove our blindness—blindness to our need of a Savior. Through the Holy Spirit He will point out the areas of sin in our life, and lead us to repentance, forgiveness, and a deeper walk with Him and its deeper spiritual insights. He also promises to give relief to the oppressed, brokenhearted, and depressed.

The last part of verse 8 tells us that "the Lord loves the righteous." No one is righteous apart from Jesus. But God loves those who, recognizing their desperate need, cast their sins upon the Savior and claim His righteousness. God makes us righteous through Jesus Christ, and even that is because of His great love.

In verse 9 the psalmist returns to God's special care for the powerless.

Verse 9

"The Lord watches over the alien and sustains the fatherless and the widow, but he frustrates the ways of the wicked."

Those who are least able to defend themselves are the objects of God's special care. The prophets were preoccupied with the plight of the widowed, the orphaned, the resident alien, and the hungry. God seems to be telling us that the weak are the object of His special interest. Just as they are His special concern, so too should they be ours. Wicked people are those who take advantage of the weak, but God is determined to frustrate their evil efforts.

Napoleon's massive army frightened the citizens of Feldkirch, Austria, as it prepared to attack. The leading citizens of the town gathered to decide whether they should fight the invaders, or surrender and hopefully save the lives of as many innocent people as possible. Resistance against such a powerful army seemed futile, especially since the town had only a small militia to protect itself. Its ranks would need to be strengthened by those who were not soldiers: bakers, barbers, butchers, and storekeepers.

Because it was Easter Sunday, the leaders of the small town assembled in the church to make their all-important decision. The pastor rose and said, "Friends, we have been counting on our own strength, and apparently that has failed. As this is the day of our Lord's resurrection, let us just ring the bells, have our services as usual, and leave the matter in His hands. We know only our weakness, and not the power of God to defend us." The council had no better plan, so they accepted the pastor's suggestion, and the church bells rang.

Napoleon's army heard the bells and concluded that the Austrian army had arrived during the night to defend the town. Before the service ended, the French broke camp and left.

God defends the defenseless—He is power for the powerless.

The psalmist has shared with us the special blessings that fall upon those who place their trust in God. He also offers reasons that the Lord is worthy of our praise. Now as the psalm reaches its conclusion, the biblical author tells us that we should praise Him throughout all generations.

Verse 10
"The Lord reigns forever, your God, O Zion, for all generations. Praise the Lord."

From one generation to the next God should receive our praise. Those who praise Him will find a special relationship with Him, and that is the best blessing anyone could ever have.

Louis Albert Banks tells of an elderly Christian man who learned that he had cancer of the tongue and that he would need surgery. The man was a wonderful singer who loved to sing praises to God, and had done so for many years. When everything was ready for the operation, the man asked the doctor, "Are you sure I will never sing again?" The physician hated to give the answer, but after a delay he nodded.

The old man then sat up in his hospital bed and said, "I've had many good times singing the praises of God. And now you tell me I can never sing again. If I have one song that will be my last, it will be of gratitude

134

and praise to God."

There in the doctor's presence the man sang softly the words of Isaac Watts's hymn:

> "I'll praise my Maker while I've breath,
> And when my voice is lost in death,
> Praise shall employ my nobler power;
> My days of praise shall ne'er be past,
> While life, and thought, and being last,
> Or immortality endures."

Are you hungry for more of God? Give Him your praise.

EXERCISES:

❖ Revisit the passages we used in the exercises from chapter 1. After reading each text, identify a characteristic of God for which to praise Him. Praise God for the ways you, your family, and your church have been blessed by that attribute.
- Exodus 34:5-7
- 2 Chronicles 2:5, 6
- Psalm 145:8, 9
- Psalm 147:3-9
- Malachi 3:6
- Mark 10:27
- James 1:17
- 1 John 4:8

❖ Read Psalms 146 through 150, using them as prayers of praise. Following those models, write your own prayers of praise to God.

❖ Sing hymns and choruses of praise during times of personal worship. The angels sing their praise before God's throne, and so should we. Make singing an integral part of your offerings of praise before God.

❖ Offer prayers of praise while engaging in the mundane tasks of life. Praise God while mowing the lawn, vacuuming the carpet, sweeping the floor, washing dishes, or changing diapers. Learn to praise God in every moment of life.

CHAPTER 13

Fear God

(Psalm 76)

When Teddy Roosevelt was a child, he was terrified of the Madison Square church. The child refused to set foot inside the church unless accompanied by an adult. When asked why, the boy replied, "I'm afraid of the zeal." According to Teddy, the "zeal" crouched in dark corners of the church, waiting to pounce on unsuspecting children.

His mother asked what the zeal was, and Teddy replied that he thought it was a very large animal—something like an alligator or a dragon. He had heard the minister read about the animal from the Bible.

She took a concordance and begin to read to her son all the passages that contained the word "zeal," until suddenly, very excited, he told her to stop at John 2:17: "And his disciples remembered that it was written, The zeal of thine house hath eaten me up" (KJV).

People are still afraid to come near the "zeal" of the Lord. Perhaps their reaction is in some ways wise. We generally think of fear as a negative thing. It can cause people to do things that they would never do under normal circumstances, or prevent them from doing things that they know they should.

Some years ago Premier Nikita Khrushchev spoke before the Supreme Soviet. His speech severely criticized the late premier Joseph Stalin. During his talk someone from the audience passed along a note: "What were you doing when Stalin committed all these atrocities?"

"Who sent that note?" Khrushchev shouted when he read it.

Not a person stirred.

"I'll give him one minute to stand up!"

No one moved.

136

"All right, I'll tell you what I was doing. I was doing exactly what the writer of this note was doing—exactly nothing! I was afraid to be counted!"

Fear can paralyze us, stopping us from acting positively to correct injustices.

Although Scripture usually speaks of fear in the negative, at times the Bible presents it as a commendable thing. It tells us that we must fear God. But we don't like to think about it, and we certainly don't think of fearing Him as a key element in satisfying our hunger for God.

Usually Scripture tells us that we are to live without fear. The most frequently repeated negative command of Scripture is "fear not." Jesus assures us that He has not given us a "spirit of fear" (2 Tim 1:7, KJV).

Why then, in light of all of this, does the Bible deem the fear of God a good thing? Why does it tell us that "the fear of the Lord is the beginning of wisdom" (Ps. 111:10)?

To find answers to such questions, we turn to Psalm 76.

Psalm 76:1–4

"For the director of music. With stringed instruments. A psalm of Asaph. A song. In Judah God is known; his name is great in Israel. His tent is in Salem, his dwelling place in Zion. There he broke the flashing arrows, the shields and the swords, the weapons of war."

I have traveled through much of the world, and I find that most people believe in God. What they disagree on is who that god is and what that deity is like. Truthfully, unless God chooses to reveal Himself, He cannot be known. God revealed Himself to Israel through the prophets and through the inspired writings of Scripture. He had a visible manifestation of Himself in the Shekinah glory that rested above the ark of the covenant in the Most Holy Place of the Temple.

Every other country of that day worshipped gods, but the true God had made an intentional, exclusive, and detailed revelation of Himself in Israel. That is why Jesus said to the Samaritan woman He met at the well, "You Samaritans worship what you do not know; we worship what we do know" (John 4:22).

The psalmist was accurate in declaring that Judah and Israel were the places God was known. Verse 2 says that God's "tent is in Salem," describing the nature and location of His dwelling. The word translated as "tent" is actually "lair." The picture is that of God as a crouched lion, ready to pounce on His enemies. Here is no "gentle Jesus, meek and mild." Lions are fierce, unpredictable, and unstoppable. Yet it is the picture that God has painted of Himself.

We think of the New Testament's portrayal of Satan as "a roaring lion, . . . seeking whom he may devour" (1 Peter 5:8, KJV). In this psalm God also depicts Himself as a lion. The Lord is not some kindly old man who is pretty much happy with us no matter what we do. Rather, He is someone to reckon with.

Verses 4-6

"You are resplendent with light, more majestic than mountains rich with game. Valiant men lie plundered, they sleep their last sleep; not one of the warriors can lift his hands. At your rebuke, O God of Jacob, both horse and chariot lie still."

Asaph wrote this psalm in celebration of the defeat that Sennacherib, the king of Assyria, experienced. Sennacherib invaded Israel, laying siege to Jerusalem, and sent a message to King Hezekiah, demanding his surrender. The Assyrian monarch recounted how he had already subdued many larger, stronger cities. They too had prayed to their gods, and had found their deities helpless to protect them against him. In essence Sennacherib defied Hezekiah's God, the only true God.

Judah's king went into the Temple to pray for deliverance from and judgment against the Assyrian invader. God sent the prophet Isaiah to announce Sennacherib's defeat. That very night the angel of the Lord put to death 185,000 Assyrian soldiers. When the Assyrian king awoke the next morning, he discovered that most of his army was dead, so he retreated to Nineveh, a broken man.

The psalmist reminds us of this story to illustrate that God is the righteous judge whose judgment will fall on those who defy Him. Mighty kings and strong warriors cannot stand against His anger. God alone is holy, just, all-powerful, and righteous. How will we resist such a deity? We will not perish only as we submit to His reign and Him cover us with the blood of His Son.

Many today see God as a kindly old man who loves too much ever to punish anyone for their misdeeds. Scripture tells a different tale. It declares that our holy God will not tolerate rebellion against His rule and reign. Let's examine four important teachings from Psalm 76.

The first teaching is that *God alone is to be feared.*

Verse 7

"You alone are to be feared. Who can stand before you when you are angry?"

I know people who are afraid of closed-in places, spiders, heights, rejection, intimacy, sickness, and death. Asaph tells us that none of those fears measure up to a proper fear of God's judgment. Scripture warns of a great final verdict, during which He will bring every secret out into the light. No one will escape it. Our God is holy, and holiness cannot abide sin. Sin must be eradicated, and He is determined to do that very thing.

Often I hear people complain of the injustices that occur on our planet. Children suffer and die; the innocent perish while the wicked flourish. All such injustices will cease when God erases evil from the earth. Those who persist in evil must fear this holy God. He and He alone is to be feared.

The second teaching is that *every mouth will be silenced by God's judgment.*

Verse 8

"From heaven you pronounced judgment, and the land feared and was quiet."

No one will have any excuse for sin. Those who reject God will have no one to blame but themselves. Ultimately He will hold everyone accountable.

A third teaching is that *God's judgment is a mixture of wrath and mercy.*

Verse 9

". . . when you, O God, rose up to judge, to save all the afflicted of the land."

Those who reject God will endure His wrath, but those who humbly confess their sins before Him will receive mercy.

When God defeated Sennacherib, He did so as a judgment against the monarch's arrogance before the true God. However, God destroyed Sennacherib's army as an act of grace for His people, Israel. The Lord shows mercy to those who have trusted Him. When He executes the final judgment at the end of time, it will be wrath mixed with mercy. His wrath will forever eradicate sin while his mercy will forever save repentant sinners.

The fourth teaching is that *even His wrath will glorify God.*

Verse 10

"Surely your wrath against men brings you praise, and the survivors of your wrath are restrained."

One interpretation of the word "wrath" is that of "separation." Those who rebel against a holy God will find themselves cut off from Him. The wrath of God eliminates injustice and everything unholy. He reserves His wrath for those who refuse to repent and live in harmony with His will. Those who have claimed Jesus as Savior and Lord will not experience the wrath of God, but will be restrained in their propensity to sin.

Countries that have a strong rule of law protect the rights of the weak against those who are strong enough to force their will on others. In fact, it is because we so often see the guilty go free, or we see unequal justice meted out, that we find ourselves with a lack of respect for the judicial system.

Our heavenly Judge never gives unequal justice. Those who refuse to repent will receive God's wrath—they will be removed from His presence. Now that we understand these four teachings, what should we do?

Verses 11, 12

"Make vows to the Lord your God and fulfill them; let all the neighboring lands bring gifts to the One to be feared. He breaks the spirit of rulers; he is feared by the kings of the earth."

We are to commit our lives to God, receive grace through Jesus, and live in harmony with the divine will.

Asaph concludes his teaching about the fear of God by calling us to a loving, obedient relationship with Him, because our worst terror is that of separation from Him. We are to be so in love with God that the greatest fear of our lives is that we would ever be forced to be away from Him whose love endures forever. It is truly a wise thing to fear God.

Many years ago the king of Hungary became severely depressed. In an attempt to relieve his depression, he sent for his brother, a good-natured, happy-go-lucky, and rather shallow prince. The monarch revealed to his brother the source of his depression. He said that he had recently come to the realization that he was a great sinner. The king was afraid to meet a holy God in judgment.

The prince laughed at the confession and told his brother that he was taking life too seriously. His reaction grieved the king, who had been expecting some emotional support. The monarch decided to teach his foolish brother a lesson.

In those days it was the custom for the executioner to sound a trumpet as he stood at a person's door before he took them to their death. The king sent the executioner, in the dead of night, to his brother's house. The executioner sounded his distinctive blast from his horn.

The prince realized with horror what was happening. The executioner seized the prince and hurried the pale, trembling frame into the king's presence. Terrified, the prince fell on his knees before his brother and begged for mercy. "Tell me how I have offended you," he pleaded, "and I will make amends."

It was the reaction the king had desired to create. "My brother," he said, "if the sight of a human executioner is so terrible to you, shall not I, having grievously offended God, fear to be brought before the judgment seat of Christ?" The king, and now the prince, had learned the value of a healthy fear of God.

Asaph had discovered the same thing centuries earlier. In Psalm 76 he declared that since God had delivered Israel from the Assyrians, they owed Him their allegiance. They had called upon the Lord, and He had saved them. Now they owed Him their worship.

God has redeemed us through the sacrifice of His Son, Jesus. His death pays the penalty for our sins, thus freeing us from divine wrath. However, it does not release us from all obligations to God. We are to obey Him—to fear God. The fear of God grows out of a recognition of His holiness. Our transcendent God is beyond human understanding.

A. W. Tozer observes that "we cannot grasp the true meaning of the divine holiness by thinking of someone or something very pure and then raising the concept to the highest degree we are capable of. God's holiness is not simply the best we know infinitely bettered. We know nothing like the divine holiness. It stands apart, unique, unapproachable, incomprehensible and unattainable. The natural man is blind to it. He may fear God's power and admire His wisdom, but His holiness he cannot even imagine."

God defies all comparisons. We have no point of reference when it comes to grasping Him and His holiness. When we do catch just a glimpse of the otherness of God, it naturally fills our hearts with fear.

We find an example of this in a story we find in Mark 4. Jesus had been teaching the crowds gathered on the shore of the Sea of Galilee. The lake, about 700 feet below sea level, fills a basin surrounded by hills. Masses of air can suddenly and rapidly slide down the slopes, producing turbulent weather. At such times, that little body of water can become particularly fierce and threatening to any vessels that happen to be on it.

EVERY GOOD THING

At the end of the day Jesus was exhausted from His work. When evening came, he said to his disciples, "Let us go over to the other side" (Mark 4:35). He and the disciples got into a little fishing boat and set off for the other side of the lake. Not only was this a faster and less-difficult way to travel, but it would also provide the 13 weary souls some measure of privacy and rest. In fact, Jesus was so tired that soon after the disciples had pushed away from shore, He fell fast asleep.

During the night a terrible storm blew up. Even though some of the disciples were experienced fishermen, they were unable to cope with the waves created by its fury, and they realized that they would soon perish. After what seemed like hours of bailing, someone noticed that Jesus was still asleep in the bottom of the boat. "Teacher, don't you care if we drown?" they exclaimed (verse 38).

It was not so much a question as an accusation. What they were suggesting was that He lacked compassion—that He didn't actually care about their difficult circumstances. Jesus responded by doing something that was completely unpredictable. Getting up, He commanded the wind and the waves to be still. Christ spoke directly to nature, and it obeyed. Immediately, the wind and waves calmed. The surface of the lake became as smooth as glass. He controlled the forces of nature by the sound of His voice.

The disciples had been fearful for their lives. They had believed that they were going to die that night. That kind of fear is gut-wrenching. After they witnessed His power over nature, they responded in an interesting way. "They were terrified and asked each other, 'Who is this? Even the wind and the waves obey him!'" (verse 41).

It is not surprising that the storm and the sea should frighten the disciples. Any of us would have had the same reaction. But once the danger had passed, we might expect that their fear would subside with the wind and the waves. But that is not what happened. Instead, it actually increased. The disciples found something in the power of Jesus that was far more frightening than anything they had ever encountered in nature. He was unlike anything or anyone they had ever known. Jesus transcended everything they had ever seen. When the disciples witnessed Him taming nature, they got a glimpse of a holy God, and it scared them to death. They feared this deity.

True wisdom begins when we catch a glimpse of a holy God and respond with reverence, awe, and even fear. This God will not allow evil to inhabit His universe for long. He is determined to do something about it, and He has the power to accomplish anything He wishes. Those who are

142

foolish enough to attempt to stand in His way are in for a terrible shock. They will encounter God's strength in ways they never dreamed possible.

The great leader of the Reformation, Martin Luther, understood something of God's transcendence. When Luther became a priest and celebrated his first Mass in 1507, he trembled so much that he nearly dropped the bread and cup. In fact, he became so terrified of the presence of Christ through the sacrament that he tried to run from the altar.

Today when so many people regard God so lightly, perhaps it is time to take a lesson from Luther and learn to fear God. The fear of God is something that should characterize His people as long as we are on the planet. John the revelator relays God's last warning message to planet earth in Revelation 14.

Revelation 14:6, 7
"Then I saw another angel flying in midair, and he had the eternal gospel to proclaim to those who live on the earth—to every nation, tribe, language and people. He said in a loud voice, 'Fear God and give him glory, because the hour of his judgment has come. Worship him who made the heavens, the earth, the sea and the springs of water.'"

This message combines the "eternal gospel" with the command to "fear God." The gospel is the solution to divine wrath, for those who accept the gospel will never be separated from God. Obedience to the command to "fear God" will characterize those who receive this message during earth's last hour.

Why are we commanded to fear Him? God is a loving Father who cares for His children. As our Father, He knows the difficulties we face and longs to protect us from them, just as any loving human father would. Therefore, He teaches His children the fear of the Lord for their protection. Psalm 34:11 declares, "Come, my children, listen to me; I will teach you the fear of the Lord." Psalm 147 sheds more light on this subject. "The Lord delights in those who fear him, who put their hope in his unfailing love" (verse 11). God's "unfailing love" is a devoted, redeeming love.

As we have seen already, the fear mentioned here is not negative. It is a reminder that although we are saved by the grace of God through the blood of Jesus, we do not have license to do as we please.

As a child I loved my parents, but when I had been disobedient, I dreaded seeing them. I feared the day of reckoning that awaited my misdeeds. That fear was healthy. How do we live in this fear? Psalm 118:4 tells us: "Let those who fear the Lord say: 'His love endures forever.'"

The passage explains that we are to show the fear of God by living in His never-ending love and declaring that love to all. His never-ending, unfailing love demonstrates that He is a good God. Our only fear is that we would ever find ourselves separated from Him.

Oswald Chambers observes that "the remarkable thing about fearing God is that when you fear God you fear nothing else, whereas if you do not fear God you fear everything else."

Instead of a paralyzing fear, it is an enabling one. It protects us from sin, and it reminds us that our only real fear is the thought of losing a God who loves us so much! A tremendous gift, the fear of God brings us peace and offers us a glimpse of a transcendent God who loves us too much ever to let us go.

EXERCISES:

❖ Ben Patterson has written that "the Bible sees no conflict between fearing God and loving and trusting Him. Amazingly, when Jesus wants to calm our fears, He tells us to first fear God." With this in mind, read these texts: 2 Chronicles 19:7-9; Job 28:28; Psalm 2:11; 19:9; 33:8; 34:11; 111:10; Proverbs 1:7; 2:5; 9:10; 10:27; 14:26, 27; 15:33; 16:6; Ecclesiastes 12:13; Isaiah 11:2, 3; 33:6; Acts 9:31; 2 Corinthians 5:11; Philippians 2:12; Revelation 14:6, 7. Ask God to show you how fearing Him can calm your fears.

❖ Make it your practice to come into a house of worship in silent reverence. Demonstrate awe, respect, reverence, and fear as you enter the presence of our holy God.

❖ Read Isaiah 6. What does the chapter teach you about God's holiness? How can it serve as a model for worshipping Him?

❖ Pray that God will give you a fear of Him that will make you show reverence and will help you to avoid sin.

CHAPTER 14

Bible Study

(Psalm 119)

John Wycliffe was a man devoted to the Scriptures. In a day when most religious leaders thought it was a useless endeavor to teach the Bible to the common people, he said, "The Sacred Scriptures are the property of the people, and one which no one should be allowed to wrest from them. . . . Christ and His apostles converted the world by making known the Scriptures to men in a form familiar to them, . . . and I pray with all my heart, that, through doing the things contained in this book, we may all together come to the everlasting life."

Wycliffe put a lot of emphasis on preaching the Word and on doing it well. While at Oxford he attracted many enthusiastic supporters through his energetic preaching and teaching. His reputation for exegetical teaching—for letting the Bible speak for itself—spread across the land. His sermons were powerful. Believing that preaching was the most important duty of a minister, he was critical of pastors who let others preach for them. Before long his followers numbered in the hundreds, and became known as Lollards, a term that may have come from an old Dutch word meaning "mumbler of prayers." Some believed that they received their name because the Word of God was always on their lips.

By 1395 the Lollards had developed into a movement that stressed a Bible-based religion, the availability of the Bible to the common person, and good preaching. Wycliffe and the Lollards became a small reformation that began about 100 years before Martin Luther.

In May of 1378 the authorities put the teachings of John Wycliffe on trial. Eventually they condemned and excommunicated him. Although he believed he would be executed for his teachings, they did allow him to retire to a small town, where he worked on his translation of the Bible into English. When you read your English Bible today, you owe much to him.

Historians have called Wycliffe "the Morning Star of the Reformation" because of his insistence that the Bible was the only legitimate authority for faith and practice. Why was he so devoted to Scripture that he would risk his life to bring its words to the general public? The only way to know for certain is to read the Bible for yourself.

With that in mind we turn now to Psalm 119, a psalm that celebrates Scripture itself. Psalm 119 is known as the longest one in the Bible. It contains 176 verses. The psalm is an elaborate acrostic poem divided into 22 stanzas, one for each letter of the Hebrew alphabet. Each of the first eight verses begins with the first letter of the Hebrew alphabet, each of the next eight verses begins with the second letter of the Hebrew alphabet, and so on.

The theme of the psalm is the Word of God. With few exceptions each verse refers to the Bible. The psalm uses several synonyms for Scripture: law, word, rulings or ordinances, testimonies, commandments, statutes, precepts or charges, and sayings or promises. The entire psalm is a celebration of Scripture and its benefits for the reader.

Bible commentator James Montgomery Boice tells the story of George Wishart, a bishop of Edinburgh during the seventeenth century. The bishop, along with his patron, the marquis of Montrose, had been sentenced to death. It was the custom in that day to allow a condemned man the right to request that a psalm be sung prior to the execution. Expecting a pardon, Wishart, in an effort to stall for time, requested Psalm 119. The psalm was about two-thirds complete when a pardon arrived, thus sparing the lives of him and Montrose.

I would imagine that Psalm 119 became Wishart's favorite psalm after that event. It has become the favorite of many others for an entirely different reason. This incredible psalm teaches us that the Bible is a wonderful source for satisfying our hunger for the living God.

Psalm 119:1-3

"[Aleph] Blessed are they whose ways are blameless, who walk according to the law of the Lord. Blessed are they who keep his statutes and seek him with all their heart. They do nothing wrong; they walk in his ways."

We might translate the word "blessed" today as "happy." Therefore, the psalm would begin, "Happy are they whose ways are blameless, who walk according to the law of the Lord."

146

Happiness is a common goal. The author of our country's Declaration of Independence penned that an inalienable right of human beings was "the pursuit of happiness," a desire shared by people of every land. The psalmist tells us that we will find happiness through a life of obedience to the Bible. The phrase "law of the Lord," you will remember, is a synonym for the Bible. Therefore, those who live according to the teachings of Scripture will find true happiness.

Verse 2 tells us, however, that living in accordance with the Bible is not just some outward behavior. It is much more, for those who do so must "seek him with all their heart." Here we come to the real purpose of Bible study. Scriptural study is not for proving some doctrinal point, although that will certainly happen as a by-product. The apostle Paul tells us that Scripture will establish sound doctrine, so that is a legitimate use. It is not, however, the primary intent.

The ultimate goal of all study of the Bible is to seek the face of God. This is true spirituality—hungering and thirsting after God with all our heart. We search the Bible to know Him.

The Bible is the primary source of information about God. It is the preeminent tool He has chosen through which to reveal Himself to us. Therefore, all study of the Bible should first and foremost disclose the Father and His Son to us. God's love letter to the objects of His affection, it enables us to know the One who created and redeemed us. When we seek and know God, then we "do nothing wrong." Knowing and living in Jesus keeps us from sin. A life in Him is a life of obedience—a sinless life.

But it is not enough to know the Bible, although this is certainly vital. We must also live the Bible. The only way to do that is to know and trust its Author. He enables us to live His life as revealed in His Word. While we are unhappy because we sin, knowing and living God's Word will keep us from sin, thus making us happy. The key is to walk in God's will.

Verses 4-6

"You have laid down precepts that are to be fully obeyed. Oh, that my ways were steadfast in obeying your decrees! Then I would not be put to shame when I consider all your commands."

God expects obedience from His children, not because He is harsh and demanding, but because He loves us and desires the best for us. We are like children who do not always recognize the best. God is the parent who sees the big picture and directs us in the ways that will produce happiness and minimize misery.

The only way to obey God's law is through the grace of Jesus. We do not have the ability to do what is right. But God, through His Son Jesus, enables us to obey His commands. It is Christ living in us that produces obedience.

Verses 9–11

"[Beth] How can a young man keep his way pure? By living according to your word. I seek you with all my heart; do not let me stray from your commands. I have hidden your word in my heart that I might not sin against you."

If we are to honor God, we must give ourselves to His Word. We must read it, learn it, and live by it. The psalmist tells us that it should begin when we are still young. We should teach our children to know and love the Bible. It wouldn't hurt if they saw Mom and Dad reading the Bible every now and then. More important, we must help our children learn how to make life decisions in accordance with Bible principles. That is still another means of satisfying our hunger for God. A study of the Bible is one important method of seeking and becoming like Him. Verse 11 tells us that knowing and living the Bible will keep us from sin.

Verse 11

"I have hidden your word in my heart that I might not sin against you."

How do we hide the Word of God in the heart? Verse 13 tells us that we are to speak the words of Scripture out loud.

Verse 13

"With my lips I recount all the laws that come from your mouth."

While reading the words of the Bible silently has value, there is an even greater power in saying them aloud, even if there is no one else in the room. Reading the Bible aloud gives the words new life and meaning. Research has revealed that we remember something better when we say it out loud. It is also important to read the words of Scripture repeatedly. Once is rarely enough. Repetition is the best teacher.

John Bunyan, who wrote *Pilgrim's Progress*, commented, "Read the Bible, and read it again, and do not despair of help to understand something of the will and mind of God, though you think they are fast locked up from you. Neither trouble yourself, though you may not have commentaries and expositions; pray and read, and read and pray; for a little from God is better than a great deal from man."

Verse 15 tells us that, like John Wycliffe's Lollards, we are to meditate on the words of Scripture.

Verse 15
"I meditate on your precepts and consider your ways."

One form of meditation involves softly repeating the words of Scripture again and again until they become a part of our being.

James M. Gray said that when he was a young Bible teacher he was impressed by the peace and spiritual poise of a friend. Gray asked the man the secret of his peace and confidence. The friend explained that while on vacation he had sat down and read all six chapters of Ephesians. The book had his attention, so he read it all again. He continued to read the book repeatedly until he had gone through it 15 times.

"When I arose to go into the house," the friend said. "I was in possession of Ephesians; or better yet, it was in possession of me. I had the feeling that I had been lifted up to sit together in heavenly places with Christ Jesus—a feeling that was new to me." Read the Bible constantly and allow it to change your life today.

Early in 1945 advance troops of the U.S. Army entered Shimabuku, Okinawa. The small town had suffered from an artillery shelling, but when an Army patrol came into the village compound, the GIs were shocked. Two little old men, bowing low, greeted them. The soldiers summoned an interpreter.

After a short conversation the interpreter announced, "Seems we're being welcomed as 'fellow Christians.' One says he's the mayor of the village; the other's the schoolmaster. That's a Bible the older one has in his hand."

Guided by the two old men, the soldiers toured the village. Every other town the Americans had entered had been filled with bewildered and despairing people, but these villagers greeted the soldiers with smiles and dignified bows.

The two men showed the Americans their spotless homes, their terraced, fertile, and neat fields, their storehouses and granaries, and their prized sugar mill. They said that they had met only one other American, many years earlier. "Because he was a Christian," the interpreter explained, "they assume we are, too—though they can't quite understand why we came in shooting."

Thirty years before, an American missionary on his way to Japan had paused at the little town, staying only long enough to make a pair of converts, the two old men who had greeted the American troops. He had left them a Japanese translation of the Bible and had encouraged them to live by it. In addition, the missionary taught them two hymns: "Fairest Lord Jesus" and "All Hail the Power of Jesus' Name."

They'd had no contact with any Christian since. Yet during those 30 years, guided by the Bible, they had managed to create a Christian community. They'd adopted the Ten Commandments as the town's legal code and the Sermon on the Mount as their guide to social conduct. The Bible was the chief literature taught in their school.

The inhabitants of this town respected human dignity and accepted the rights and responsibilities of citizenship. As a result, they had no jail, no brothel, no drunkenness, and no divorce. Their worship services consisted of the reading of Scripture and the singing of the only two hymns they knew. Because they had only one copy of Scripture, they treated it with great reverence even though it was dog-eared from 30 years of use.

Though everyone had forgotten the missionary's name, the villagers did remember his parting words. "Study this Book well. It will give you strong faith. . . . And when your faith in God is strong, everything is strong."

No wonder the psalmist wrote:

Verse 16
"I delight in your decrees; I will not neglect your word."
As we heed these words and study the Bible, our lives change.

Many have tried to discredit this book, but all have failed. During the French Revolution the French philosopher Voltaire wrote that in 100 years the Bible would become a forgotten book. But a century after he made that statement the Bible was, as it is today, the number one best-selling book in the world. So much for the death of the Bible!

Others have tried to discredit the Bible as a historically accurate document. They have questioned its stories and claimed that it did not agree with known historical records. However, every year brings new archaeological discoveries that confirm Scripture's accuracy. To date, some 25,000 archaeological sites relate, in some way or other, to the Bible.

Ancient secular historians agreed with the record of Scripture in amazing detail and consistency. Another proof of the reliability of Scripture is fulfilled prophecy.

Some have questioned how we can be certain that the Bible we have today is the same as when composed by the prophets and apostles. After all, it has been copied, translated, and retranslated throughout the centuries. Isn't it possible that mistakes have crept in or that someone has changed the text? Those who verify works of antiquity as being accurate and reliable representations of what had been written so long ago apply several tests. I did a Google search recently and found this information at http://faithfacts.gospelcom.net. Another helpful site is www.abounding joy.com with a page entitled, "Help for Skeptics."

First, in verifying an ancient document, scholars ask how many ancient copies of the manuscript exist today. The New Testament has 24,000 known copies or portions of copies. Compare that with Homer's *Iliad*, which has 643 ancient manuscripts. Most ancient documents have fewer than 25 ancient copies preserved today. Only five copies of Aristotle's works and seven copies of Plato's works have survived. That is minuscule in comparison to the number of ancient biblical manuscripts.

Second, it is important to know how close to the original date of composition the existing copies were made. The New Testament has extant copies produced from 60 to 135 years after the originals. So short an interval between the original and the ancient copies is unheard-of in documents of antiquity. The oldest known examples of the works of Plato were copied some 1,250 years after he composed the original manuscripts.

The written record of the life of Jesus came into being closer to the events themselves than for any other personality of antiquity. The oldest existing account of the life of Buddha did not appear until 500 years after his death. Why is it, then, that if the Bible is the most thoroughly documented work of antiquity the world has ever known, people question its authenticity while accepting the works of Plato as legitimate?

Third, it is important to know if those ancient manuscripts agree with each other. The evidence for the New Testament is impressive. Considering all the ancient copies that survive today, only .2 percent of the verses of the New Testament are even in question. That is an amazing degree of consistency from one copy to another! The New Testament is more than 25 times more accurately copied than the *Iliad*, considered to be one of the best preserved works of antiquity.

The internal consistency of the Bible is another amazing proof of its reliability. The Bible is a collection of 66 books composed by more than 40 authors during a period of 1,500 to 1,600 years. Most of the authors did not know each other, and many did not have the writings of the other biblical authors available at the time they worked. Yet the Bible fits together beautifully and, when properly understood, does not contradict itself.

151

But the most amazing proof of the reliability of the Bible is the fact that the power of its words have changed so many lives. The psalmist declares:

Verse 11
"I have hidden your word in my heart that I might not sin against you."

I recommend to you a study of God's Word, the Holy Bible. It will change your life!

If you have had difficulty knowing how to do this, I'd like to offer a few suggestions. While there are many different ways to explore the Bible, the very best way is a verse-by-verse and book-by-book study. It will really enable you to dig down into Scripture so that you can allow it to change your life.

First, choose a readable and understandable version of Scripture. Several modern language translations are excellent. I preach, primarily, from the New International Version. It is written in today's English and is highly readable. However, you may prefer other equally good translations.

Next, decide on a book of the Bible to study. I would suggest that you begin with either Psalms or one of the Gospels: Matthew, Mark, Luke, or John. If you read Matthew or Luke, you might want to skip the genealogies for now. That's where it says that so-and-so was the parent of so-and-so and on and on. All of that is important, but not for our purposes of devotional Bible study.

Select a short passage of Scripture. If you begin with Matthew, start with Matthew 1:18. Read six to 12 verses a day. For example, go through Matthew 1:18-25. The next day you will read Matthew 2:1-12, and then follow the same pattern each day.

Once you have decided what to read, follow this procedure.

First, pray that God will lead you in your study and will open your eyes to truth.

Second, read the passage quickly to get the feel of it.

Third, read the passage again, this time out loud, in order to hear as well as see the words.

Fourth, read the passage again, asking yourself, "What does this tell me about God/Jesus?" Jot your thoughts down in a notebook.

Fifth, read the passage again, keeping in mind the question "What does this tell me about how God treats people?" Again, write down your thoughts and observations.

Sixth, read the passage again in light of "What does this tell me that

God wants me to do today?" Again, record your thoughts.

If time permits, look up any words you may think are important or whose meaning you may not understand. You can use a Bible dictionary for this, though even just a good English dictionary will provide some insights.

Next, quickly commit a word, a short phrase, or a verse to memory and repeat that short section of Scripture to yourself all day long. It is a form of Christian meditation that we can do any time and anywhere.

Finally, close your time of study with a prayer of reception and surrender. Give yourself to God and to whatever He wants to do in your life that day.

That's it. It's not complicated. When time is limited, shorten the procedure by skipping a step or two. However, you will achieve the best results by following every step. Make it a part of your daily routine and see how the Word of God can change your life.

EXERCISES:

- ❖ Prayerfully commit to spending 15 minutes each day in Bible study. Expand the time as you grow more proficient in it.
- ❖ Using the method explained above, begin a study of one of the Gospels. Follow this method until you have completed the book you selected. Then begin the process on another book of your choosing.
- ❖ Make knowing Jesus the goal of your study. Devotional study is not primarily designed to prove some point of doctrine, as important as that may be. It seeks to reveal Jesus Christ and to make us more like Him.

An ancient method of Bible reading that allows us to read for relationship is called Lectio Divina (translated "divine [or sacred] reading"). Much of what I will share about it appears either in Ruth Haley Barton's book *Sacred Rhythms* or in *Contemplative Bible Reading,* by Richard Peace. This approach dates back to the earliest days of the Christian church. It involves reading and meditation on Scripture in four movements. It does not attempt to analyze Scripture or discover doctrinal truth from the passage. Rather it is a method of reading for relationship with God. While not intended to take the place of other forms of Bible study, it can be an essential supplement to them or even a follow-up to more traditional Bible study methods.

First, choose a passage of Scripture no longer than six to eight verses in length. Begin with a time of silent preparation ("silencio"), during which you come in touch with your desire to hear from God.

Next, read the passage through ("lectio"). Read it once or twice slowly, focusing on a word or phrase that especially strikes you. Such a word or phrase will stand out from all the rest in the sense that you either resonate with it or you find that it stimulates a sense of resistance. Once you have found that word or phrase, spend a brief period of silence during which you savor or repeat it without trying to figure out what it means or understand why you have reacted to it as you have.

The second movement is to reflect ("meditatio"). It is now time to meditate on whatever you have chosen. Read the passage again and then reflect on why the word or phrase has caught your attention or why it produced the response it did. Ask yourself, "Why did I need to hear this word today?" or "Where am I in this story and what emotions am I experiencing as I allow myself to live it?"

The third movement is to respond ("oratio"). What invitation or challenge does God present to you in the word or phrase? How do you respond to His invitation?

A part of our response to the word that God has given us will be a prayer. Take time to offer a prayer of response. Be completely open and honest during it. If the word that God has given you has opened some area of pain, pour it out freely before your Lord. Or if what this word calls for seems a bit too much for you, be truthful with God. Your prayer may contain such phrases as "You can't really mean for me to do that, can You?" or "God, this is too much for me!"

Once the reaction has subsided, it is time for the fourth movement. It is simply to rest in God ("contemplatio"). As you become aware that He is the one who will enable you to respond, you can simply rest in Him and in His strength. Rest in His peace. Resolve to carry this word with you throughout the day and to live it out in your life ("incarnatio"). Contemplate it throughout the day and seek deeper meaning in it.

We can summarize Lectio Divina as: prepare, quietly coming into the presence of God with an attitude of expectation; read, listening for the word or phrase that arrests your attention; reflect, meditating on how it touches your life; respond, determining what God seeks from you in deed or attitude; rest, trusting that God will supply whatever power you may need for the proper response; and resolve, living out this word in your daily life.

More Spiritual Habits

What I have referred to as spiritual habits, Richard Foster, Dallas Willard, and others call spiritual disciplines. Other phrases used for spiritual habits are "the rule of life" and "spiritual rhythms." All of these terms refer to the same thing: behaviors designed to reproduce the character of Christ in us. They are designed to help us love both God and others more every day. But they are not measurements of holiness. We are never to judge anyone by their spiritual habits. Spiritual habits are simply tools to make us more like Jesus.

The ones we have looked at in this book are not a complete listing. Such habits as fasting, solitude, service, and celebration are of inestimable value in forming a character like that of Jesus. For further study, I recommend John Ortberg's book, *The Life You've Always Wanted,* Richard Foster's *Celebration of Discipline,* or Ruth Haley Barton's *Sacred Rhythms.* I have found all three to be of great help in my own growth in Christ. But even the habits listed in these excellent works are still not complete. In reality the list is infinite.

While space will not allow a thorough discussion of all possible spiritual habits, perhaps a brief explanation of a few additional ones will be of some value.

Fasting

As is the case with prayer, God initiates fasting. Fasting focuses solely on God and is for the purpose of bringing our will into harmony with His. It reminds us that it is not food, but God Himself that sustains us. Fasting also helps us realize that we tend to be controlled by forces other than God.

Appetite is one drive that has the potential to dominate us. But fasting helps us surrender this part of our life to His control.

When we fast, our food must be God's Word. We feast on Him through Bible study, meditation, and prayer. Every pang of hunger reminds us that we must long for God as much as we do for food. Hunger pangs serve as a reminder to pray when we are fasting. Our prayers during a fast are to be for God's will to be done, usually in one specific area of concern.

We can fast in different ways. One form is to drink only water while taking absolutely no solid food or juices. Another type of fast has been called the Daniel fast. During it we eat only fruits and vegetables, consuming no meat, sugar, or any other food.

My suggestion for fasting is to eat lunch and then not eat solid food again until lunch the following day. During those 24 hours partake of only water and juices. Allow this to be a time of focusing the mind on God. Do not tell anyone that you are fasting unless absolutely necessary. Set aside specific times for prayer. In addition, every time you feel hungry, take a few minutes to pray. This is a private matter between you and God. It is to be a time of seeking His face as well as making your request of Him.

Some people have formed the habit of fasting on a weekly basis. I find that such a practice can quickly become a form of legalism or pride for me. Generally I reserve fasting for more special times of seeking the divine will.

Solitude

One could call solitude a fast from both people and noise while feasting on God and silence. Solitude acknowledges that we have been depending upon human beings rather than God. It is a means of stilling the clamor of life while centering the life upon Him.

It may be best for you to begin by looking for moments of solitude during the day. Sometimes I wake up before the rest of the family. While still in bed, I focus my attention on God. The house is quiet, and I do not say a word. Instead, I just think, *God, please allow me to enjoy being quiet in Your presence for a few minutes.*

Others find that they can experience moments of solitude while sitting in bumper-to-bumper traffic during the morning commute. When they turn the radio off and center the life in God, they find a quiet joy of depending upon Him alone.

Try finding a quiet place in your home. My wife uses our walk-in closet as hers. She sits cross-legged on the floor for times of Bible reading, prayer, and quiet solitude. Gayle learns to let God alone become enough for her in the stillness of our closet.

Another step toward solitude is to measure our words. Most of us speak too much during the day. Try saying less while listening more. Some have tried to spend an entire day without words while focusing on the voice of the Spirit within.

It would be helpful for every Christian to spend three to four hours reevaluating life goals at least four times a year. Taking a few hours of quietness to examine where we are today and where we want to be in the future can help us gain perspective and keep us on track. Those few hours of quietness can allow God to refocus our lives according to His values.

While such brief times of solitude are helpful, we will gain the greatest benefit by taking a two- to three-day study and solitude break each year. We should spend such time in silence, Bible study, prayer, and simply experiencing God's presence. What such a retreat will accomplish is invaluable. We learn to depend upon the Lord alone, and find the strength that comes from a life centered on Him.

Service

A world in which everyone is climbing the corporate ladder, looking out for number one, or trying to get ahead desperately needs the spiritual habit of service. Service actually offers a different style of leadership. It is the one modeled by Jesus—servant leadership. Jesus, who was Lord of all, willingly became the servant of all. He is our model.

The spiritual habit of service places the needs of others ahead of our own. Some serve others in the hope that what they do will get noticed by those in authority and result in advancement. But that is not the model of service given to us by Jesus. Instead, we offer service to those from whom we have no hope of benefit. We, like Jesus, must become the servant of all.

Genuine service begins in the home. Make it your business to look for ways to share with family members and others what some have called "random acts of kindness." When possible, it is best to remain anonymous when we engage in this spiritual habit, but whether or not anonymity is possible, acts of service are to be the order of our lives.

Service takes many forms. At times we may serve by waiting in silence, without complaint. At other times we serve by silently listening. Other forms of service involve words of encouragement and affirmation. Performing menial tasks for others is the most recognized form of service, the type that Jesus offered to His disciples the night He took towel and basin to wash the feet of those who should have served Him.

Mission trips are wonderful ways to practice this habit, but we should not limit our service just to such times. It is to be the order and pattern of our lives. Every day there are those in your life whom an act of service would bless more than any sermon. Jesus' pattern of ministry was to serve others by meeting their needs and thus winning their confidence. Then He extended the invitation to follow Him.

Service enables us to practice true humility. It is a constant reminder that no hierarchy exists among the citizenry of the kingdom of heaven. All are equal in God's kingdom. The ground at the foot of the cross is level. The spiritual habit of service makes us mindful of this reality.

Celebration

Jesus began His public ministry by announcing jubilee, a biblical time of celebration.

Luke 4:18, 19

"The Spirit of the Lord is on me, because he has anointed me to preach good news to the poor. He has sent me to proclaim freedom for the prisoners and recovery of sight for the blind, to release the oppressed, to proclaim the year of the Lord's favor."

The followers of Christ are to experience a perpetual jubilee of spirit. We are to celebrate the gospel and the salvation it brings. The gospel gives us freedom from the bondage of care and concern over the things of this earth. It has freed us from the bondage of possessions and the opinions of others. God's people have been set free from the enslavement of sin. Why wouldn't we celebrate?

Paul demands that we "rejoice in the Lord always. I will say it again: Rejoice!" (Phil. 4:4).

Jesus Himself declared: "I have told you this so that my joy may be in you and that your joy may be complete" (John 15:11).

An identifying mark of the true follower of Christ is joy. God's true people in every age, and especially in this final age, will be a people of celebration. It will be both an individual and a corporate habit of His true disciples.

But how do we do it? Scripture tells us to celebrate with singing, dancing, and shouting. David danced before the Lord, and the psalms repeatedly tell us to shout to the Lord. There are times when all of these activities are appropriate for even the most conservative of Christians. After all, Scripture does command them.

Laughter is another mark of celebration. A long-faced Christian is actually an oxymoron, the greatest of all contradictions. Christians are people who have been forgiven. We have full assurance that we will live forever in pure joy in the presence of Jesus. Why wouldn't we be a people of joyous laughter?

Creativity and the appreciation of beauty are celebratory activities. God gave gifts of both in such areas as music, dance, painting, and sculpture. We should give the goodness of God expression either through using our God-given talents in the arts, or through enjoying the talents of others.

Psalm 150 is an excellent example of an experience of celebration. Music is the special area of focus for an expression of joy. It should not always sound like a funeral dirge. Nothing gives expression to joy and a spirit of celebration as music. God's people will enjoy lively, celebrative music.

Make every day a day of celebration. Live in the joy that Jesus intended you to experience. Believe it or not, this is actually a spiritual habit—a practice that brings us closer to God and satisfies our longing for Him.

Anything that helps you live a life that more closely resembles Jesus can be a spiritual habit. You can invent your own spiritual habit. Look at an area of spiritual need in your life and then think of an activity that, when made continual, meets that need.

One of the spiritual struggles I've experienced is that of a quick and sharp tongue. I have a tendency to give rapid and cutting replies whenever I feel criticized or attacked. Obviously, such a reaction does not reflect the Jesus who answered not a word when accused before Pilate and Herod. In order to become more like Jesus, I've begun to practice the spiritual habit of "the forfeiture of the right to self-defense." When someone criticizes or attacks me, I attempt to receive their criticism in silence. It is my objective to offer no defense. Instead, I seek to listen. In listening, the Holy Spirit has often been able to show me that something deeper is at work in those who so readily offer criticism. Usually, if I listen long enough, the Holy Spirit will show me some area of pain that triggered the attack. When I address the pain, I am able to be of help to my critic. Together we are often able to find the healing of the Holy Spirit.

As you can see, when spiritual habits are a part of our everyday life, we have a wonderful opportunity to grow in the grace of God. The Spirit helps us reflect more and more of the love of Jesus to our world—the goal of every spiritual habit.

It is my prayer that you will grow daily in the grace of our Lord and Savior, Jesus Christ. The Spirit will direct you to employ the spiritual habits that are most important for your personal maturing. Trust Him to lead you. He wants you to reflect His character more fully. I know that is your goal as well.

Only a fresh experience with God can quell your spiritual hunger pangs. He alone can satisfy your God hunger.

Romans 15:13

"May the God of hope fill you with all joy and peace as you trust in him, so that you may overflow with hope by the power of the Holy Spirit."

VietNAm — Buddy — honour — Mutual Respect
— Lay Life down — Deep Effection — Die
— give life

- CONFLICT RESOLUTION
- Proof Texts: Proverbs 24:16 FALL seven Times

C Closeness true to Genesis 2:24 Leave + cleave Ps 3:4
O Openess Col 3:19   29:74 Gen 30:20   Ps 2:6
U Understanding   Malach 3:14 take heed to your spirit   Ps 8:3
P Peace making I Peter 3:7 Weaker — honour wife — solution
L Loyalty   Math 19:5+6 Become one flesh.   listening
E Esteem   Mal 2:14 I cor 7:3+4
S   I Peter 3:7 companion 2:16 Hate divorce

Wife to   NO Self-Deprecation   desire to work + achieve
appreciate   Husband
- Protect + Provide
- Desire to be strong + lead + make decisions
- analyze and council
- Shoulder to shoulder friendship
- Desire for sexual intimacy

C — Conquest   desire to work + achieve   Gen 2:15
H — Hierarchy   instrument in crowd   Gen 2:18
A — authority   Desire to Protect + Provide   I Tim 5:8   Eph 5:23-25
I — INSIGHT   Desire to be strong + lead   I Tim 2:12
R — Relationship   " " analyze + council   I cor 16:13   Luke 8:14
S — sexuality   Shoulder to shoulder friendship   I Kings 2:2   Psalms 5:1, 16
    Desire for sexual Intimacy   Prov 5:19   I corinthian 7: